A TOUR WITH TEXACO

Rick Pease

4880 Lower Valley Rd. Atglen, PA 19310 USA

D1597981

This book is gratefully dedicated to my special friends, Erol and Susan Tuzcu. I had the pleasure of spending several days in West Palm Beach, Florida, with Erol and Susan taking pictures and discovering Texaco items that I did not know existed. 98% of the items in this book are from Erol's collection which was started in the 1980s. Some items were still in unopened boxes. Erol was kind enough to allow me to unpack each item (hundreds of them) and display them in a proper place on a shelf or on the wall—up and down the ladder for days, hammering, hanging, admiring, taking photographs. I love you guys.

ACKNOWLEDGMENTS

A very special thanks to the following people
for their photographs and information:

Mark Anderton, Scott Benjamin, Bob and Barbara Burke, Nick Ciovica, Mark Cioni, Pete Clarke, Howard Clayburn, Richard Eaves, Ron Hoyt, Irvin Kutzer, Kyle Moore, Gary Oelkers, Giovanni Paganoni, *Petroleum Collectibles* Archives, Erol Tuzcu, Vernon Walker, David Wallace, and the Ziesemer family.

Copyright © 1997 by Rick Pease
Library of Congress Catalog Card Number: 97-68172

All rights reserved. No part of this work may be reproduced or used in any form or by any means—graphic, electronic, or mechanical, including photocopying or information storage and retrieval systems—without written permission from the copyright holder.

Designed by Bonnie M. Hensley

ISBN: 0-7643-0360-0
Printed in China

Published by Schiffer Publishing Ltd.	In Europe, Schiffer books are distributed by
4880 Lower Valley Road	Bushwood Books
Atglen, PA 19310	84 Bushwood Lane
Phone: (610) 593-1777; Fax: (610) 593-2002	Kew Gardens
E-mail: Schifferbk@aol.com	Surrey TW9 3BQ England
Please write for a free catalog.	Phone: 44 (0)181 948-8119; Fax: 44 (0)181
This book may be purchased from the publisher.	948-3232
Please include $3.95 for shipping.	E-mail: Bushwd@aol.com

Please try your bookstore first.
We are interested in hearing from authors
with book ideas on related subjects.

CONTENTS

INTRODUCTION

The Texas Company came into being in 1901 due to the Texas oil booms generated by the Lucas oil gusher on Spindletop. Approximately 200 rivals also came into being during that same time. Many fortunes were made and lost in only a day. A number of the rivals were unable to stay in business because of the lack of management expertise. However, through the excellent leadership and energy of Joseph Stephen Cullinan and Arnold Schlet, The Texas Company emerged as a factor in the nation's oil industry.

The Texas Company was incorporated under the laws of Texas on April 7, 1902. At this time Standard Oil did 80% of the nation's oil business and a greater percentage abroad. This was a time when independent oil companies were finding it difficult to compete with Standard.

Through the years The Texas Company took many risks in order to deal with the ambiguity of a constantly changing competitive market. Nevertheless, building on the forward momentum of Mr. Cullinan and Mr. Schlet, The Texas Company became a billion-dollar corporation by 1947, and a billion-and-a-half-dollar corporation in 1951.

The following is a list of acquisitions by Texaco, Inc. (this information is taken from a 1933 Petroleum Register, The Texaco Story, Houston Geological Society).

1902 Texas Fuel Company
1917 Producers Oil Company
1928 California Petroleum Company
      Galena Signal Oil Company
1931 Majority control of Indian Refining Company was acquired January 14, and with it a refinery at Lawrenceville, Illinois. (The major reason for obtaining interest in Indian Refining was to utilize the patent on de-waxing motor oil.)
1933 Purchased an interest in Great Lakes Pipe Line Co. on May 10 (a gasoline pipe line from Oklahoma and Kansas to Illinois and neighboring states).
1936 Part ownership in the Barco Concession in Columbia was acquired.
      A 50 percent interest was purchased in California Arabian Standard Oil Company (later to become Arabian American Oil Company—ARAMCO).

A 50 percent interest was purchased in a company which held concessions in Sumatra and Java.
1942 Wellington Oil Company
1948 Purchased controlling interest in McColl-Frontenac Oil Co., Ltd.
1956 Trinidad Oil Company
1958 Seaboard Oil Company
1959 Paragon Oil Company
      The Texas Company
1961 T & L Oil
1962 TXL Oil Corporation
1983 Dome Petroleum Corporation (U.S. assets)
1984 Getty Oil Company
      Associated Oil Company (1956)
      Basin Petroleum Corporation (1980)
      Fargo Oils, Ltd. (1968)
      Lorena Oil Company
      Minnehoma Oil Company
      Mission Development (1977)
      Monday Oil Company (1946)
      Pacific Western Oil Corp. (1956)
      Penntex Petroleum Company
      Reserve Oil and Gas Company (1980)
      Rock Hill Oil Co. (1955)
      RVO Petroleum Company (1981)
      Skelly Oil Company (1977)
      Tide Water Associated Oil Company (1956)
      Tide Water Oil Company (1956)
      Tidewater Oil Company (1957)
1989 Tana Production Company

Just a few interesting tidbits:

✪ The Texas Company's first pipe line from Spindletop was completed to Garrison, Texas, on May 16, 1902.
✪ In August 1902 The Texas Company bought its first item of marine equipment—a barge.
✪ In September 1902 the first terminal was opened at Port Arthur.
✪ On December 21, 1902, the word "Texaco" was first used as a product name. The product, asphalt, was first sold in February 1903.
✪ Late in 1903, The Texas Company's refinery at Port Arthur began operation.
✪ On September 29, 1905, Texaco organized the

Continental Petroleum Company for foreign trade. Texaco had a terminal at Antwerp, Belgium.

- ✪ In 1905 the first distributing station was built at Laredo, Texas.
- ✪ In 1905 The Texas Company began to develop the foreign retail market.
- ✪ In 1906 "Texaco" was registered as a trademark.
- ✪ In 1907 Texaco began to bring Oklahoma crude by pipeline to Texas.
- ✪ In 1908, the new tanker 'Texas' went into regular service between Port Arthur and Continental ports. By 1913, the Texaco Star was visible in Europe, Latin America, Australia, Africa, and several Asian countries
- ✪ In 1908, The Texas Company moved its headquarters from Beaumont to Houston.
- ✪ In 1909, the Texaco red star with the green "T" appeared.
- ✪ The first process of putting gasoline into the tank of an auto was by means of a can and a funnel. Soon, the motorist could drive into a garage and an attendant filled the tank from a barrel with a hand pump and hose. Quickly, the underground storage tank was built, and, around 1910, the pump at the curbstone was available. These curbstone pumps are recognized as the forerunners of today's service station pumps.
- ✪ In August 1926 The Texas Corporation, a holding company, was organized.
- ✪ In 1930 Texaco-Ethyl Gasoline was placed on the market.
- ✪ In 1932 Texaco Fire Chief Gasoline was announced. The first comedy program on nationwide radio, starring Ed Wynn as the "Fire Chief", introduced Fire Chief Gasoline on the air.
- ✪ In 1933 The Texas Company purchased an interest in Great Lakes Pipe Line Company.
- ✪ In 1935 the Kaw Pipe Line Company, a crude oil pipe line in western Kansas, was organized. Texaco owned one-third of the pipe line.
- ✪ In 1936 New Texaco Motor Oil went on the market
- ✪ In 1936 the Bahrain-Caltex group of companies, (owned 50 percent by Texaco) was formed.
- ✪ In 1937 the Texas-New Mexico Pipe Line Company was formed.
- ✪ In 1938 Texaco Sky Chief Gasoline, a premium product, was introduced.
- ✪ In 1941 The Texas Corporation was dissolved and became The Texas Company.
- ✪ In 1942 Texaco, along with other major oil companies, organized War Emergency Pipelines, Inc. This was formed to build (for the Defense Plant Corporation, 1942) a 24-inch crude line and a 20-inch products line from East Texas to the Atlantic seaboard.
- ✪ In 1943, The Texas Company and seven other oil companies organized War Emergency Tankers, Inc., to operate ocean-going tankers without profit.
- ✪ In 1944, Jefferson Chemical Company, Inc., was organized by The Texas Company and American Cyanamid Company for the utilization of ethylene glycol for automotive anti-freeze purposes.
- ✪ In 1947 Texaco's European subsidiaries were sold to California Texas Oil Company, Ltd. (50% owned by Texaco).
- ✪ In 1948 Texaco PT Anti-Freeze, made from ethylene glycol, went on the market.
- ✪ In 1949 Texaco Texamatic Fluid for automatic transmissions was introduced.

TEXACO DUMP WAGON

Edward Ziesemer was born on Valentine's Day in 1904, five years before the first horse-drawn cart was built for Texaco. When Edward was thirteen, his family bought a farm in Homer Township in Illinois. He helped his dad haul milk by wagon to Joliet dairies. He not only helped his dad on the farm, he also helped other nearby farmers when they needed milk to be transported to the city. Thus began his love for wagons.

In 1929 Edward Ziesemer opened the first Texaco gas station in Homer Township. He operated the station along with his farm duties. In 1936 Edward was hired by Texaco. He said he was probably hired because of his knowledge of horses and wagons. The wagons were used to haul scrap, roofing, bricks, asphalt, and other materials to landfills and to help build roads throughout the refinery in Lockport. When he received his first paycheck from Texaco, Edward and his sweetheart, Loretta, got married.

In the 1940s when trucks replaced the wagons, Edward bought the wagons (there were two) from Texaco and displayed them proudly at his farm. Vandals destroyed one of the wagons, but the other remained on his farm until he passed it on to his daughter, Sylvia Zielke. Sylvia has been a Texaco distributor since 1975.

In 1987 Texaco asked Edward if they could display the cart at their high-rise offices in Houston. Texaco had researched the cart and found that it was the only one in existence. Knowing that Texaco would take good care of it, Edward agreed to let them have it as long as they needed it. However, in September 1996 Texaco returned the cart to the family of Edward and Loretta. Sadly, Edward Ziesemer had died in 1995—one day before Valentine's Day—but Loretta and family accepted the cart because they wanted it preserved for history.

The Ziesemer family did not consider selling it to anyone because they wanted to be sure it was taken care of—that is, they did not consider selling it until they talked to Erol Tuzcu. They felt their meeting was fate and not coincidence when they found out that Erol was born on Valentine's Day. Erol told them of his Texaco collection and his desire to have the cart on display in his museum. The Ziesemers know the cart will be taken care of and the memory of Edward Ziesemer will be preserved.

Erol, and the rest of us collectors, are grateful to Edward and Loretta Ziesemer and daughter Sylvia Zielke, and Bonnie Packley (plant manager of Lockport Refinery) for preserving bits and pieces of our past.

Edward Ziesmer and daughter Sylvia

Two-Horse Wagon
Originally Owned by

The Texas Company
and
Operated by the Team and Truck Department
at the
Lockport Refinery — Lockport, Illinois
1930's - 1940's

This wagon was used to haul: asphalt, bricks, roofing and other building materials, as well as fill for road building projects within the refinery property during the period.

This wagon was given to Texaco by Mr. Edward Ziesemer, a resident of Homer Township, Joliet, Illinois, and an employee at the Texaco Lockport Refinery from 1936 until his retirement in 1969.

Mr. Ziesemer drove this wagon pulled by a matched team of horses, June and Jane. They performed duties for the refinery's Team and Truck Department from 1936 until the early 1940's. He purchased the wagon in the 1940's since all refinery transportation duties were taken over by motor trucks.

Texaco Inc. gratefully acknowledges the gift of this wagon, in ceremonies at Texaco's Houston Headquarters. This 19th day of April, 1988.

HISTORY IN THE MAKING

Tour with Texaco

Texaco as a youngster

Texaco Exhibit in South America

Texaco Exhibit at the Dallas, Texas Fair, 1915

These photos show the size of the exhibit

Texaco Exhibit, 1933

Close-up of Ed Wynn

Texaco Exhibit, 1952, 50th Anniversary

Texaco Station, Rio de Janeiro, Brazil

Place de l'Yser Service Station, Belgium

Station in Sweden

Bulk Plant, Memphis, Tennessee

Texaco Station in Minneapolis, Minnesota

Texas Company Headquarters in Holland (Texaco House-to-House deliveries)

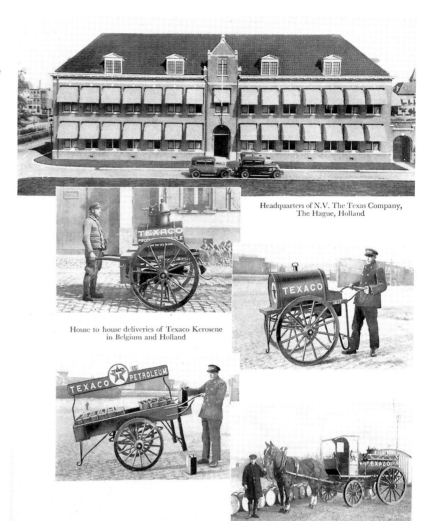

Headquarters of N.V. The Texas Company, The Hague, Holland

House to house deliveries of Texaco Kerosene in Belgium and Holland

Peddler's Tank Wagon, Holland

Kang and Kim—Korean high school boys selling Texaco Kerosene

Manufacturing "Texaco" enamel signs in the Far East

Exhibition of various articles made from "Texaco" cans and cases by ingenious Chinese

Making and Selling Texaco Products

Stations in Hong Kong and Shanghai

One of the many Texaco Filling Stations, Hong Kong, China

Filling Station, Kowloon, Hong Kong, China

One of The Texas Company (China), L. Filling Station at Shanghai

Service Station of The Texas Company, Atlanta (Georgia, U.S.A.)

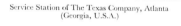

Typical Texaco Truck used in transporting barrels of lubricating oils

Below—Texaco Truck and Trailer used in hauling gasoline on the Pacific Coast. Total capacity: 6,004 gallons

Station in Atlanta—typical Texaco transport trucks

Lockport Refinery

Lockport Refinery

Horse-drawn Tank Wagon

Petrified Wood Station in Decatur, Texas (1927)

Historical Marker commissioned in 1995

TEXAS TOURIST CAMP COMPLEX

LOCAL BUSINESSMAN E.F. BOYDSTON (1888-1945) PURCHASED THIS SITE, A FORMER FEED LOT, IN 1927 FOR $400. RECOGNIZING A POTENTIAL BUSINESS OPPORTUNITY IN OFFERING SERVICES TO THE TRAVELING PUBLIC, HE BUILT A WOODEN SHED AND GAS STATION IN 1927. TRAVELERS WERE ALLOWED TO BUILD CAMP-FIRES DURING OVERNIGHT STAYS, AND BY 1931 BOYDSTON ADDED THREE WOODEN CABINS WITH GARAGES TO THE CAMP COM-PLEX. THE BUILDINGS LATER WERE FACED WITH ROCK, AND MORE CABINS AND GARAGES WERE ADDED IN 1935. THE ORIGI-NAL WOODEN GAS STATION WAS COVERED WITH PETRIFIED WOOD IN 1935 WHEN THE HIGHWAY WAS WIDENED AND RE-MAINED IN OPERATION BY THE BOYDSTON FAMILY UNTIL 1988.
THE TEXAS LUNCHROOM, A ONE-ROOM FRAME BUILDING, WAS BUILT IN 1929. RENAMED THE TEXAS CAFE IN 1935 AND FACED WITH STONE TO MATCH OTHER BUILDINGS IN THE COMPLEX, IT WAS ENLARGED TO PROVIDE SECOND-FLOOR LIVING QUARTERS. POPULAR WITH LOCAL HIGH SCHOOL AND COLLEGE STUDENTS, AS WELL AS FAMILIES AND THE TRAVELING PUBLIC, IT WAS CLOSED IN THE 1960s AFTER A HIGHWAY BYPASS BUILT WEST OF TOWN DIVERTED TRAFFIC FROM THIS AREA. THE CAFE RE-OPENED IN 1993. ONE OF THE FEW INTACT EXAMPLES OF TOURIST CAMPS BUILT THROUGHOUT TEXAS IN THE MID-20TH CENTURY, THIS PROPERTY IS SIGNIFICANT FOR ITS ASSOCIATION WITH THE EARLY DEVELOPMENT OF AUTOMOBILE TOURISM.
RECORDED TEXAS HISTORIC LANDMARK - 1995

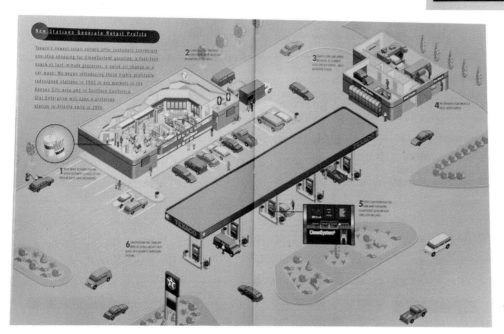

Today's Modern Texaco Star Station

Display of various Texaco Products

Sign and 5-quart Oil Can, 1937

Little Boy admiring Aviation Sign

Texaco Products display

5-gallon Fry Pump with Indian Globe and various items (restored by Rick Pease)

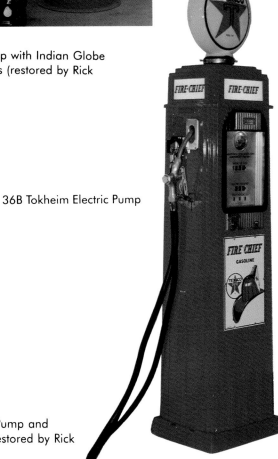

36B Tokheim Electric Pump

Martin-Schwartz Electric Pump and curb-side Sentry Pump (restored by Rick Pease)

10-gallon Fry Pump on the left, 5-gallon Fry Pump on the right

Another nice Texaco Display

Yet another nice Texaco Display

1938 Gasoline Tanker (nicknamed 'Old George')

"Old Geor[ge]

1938 TEXACO Gas

- Custom built 1938 by Butl[er]
- Rebuilt in 1990 by Terry & L[e]
- 305 Chev V-8
- 350 Turbo Transmissi[on]
- 308 Posi
- Mustang Rack & Pini[on]
- Paint & Body work by Ste[ve]
- Lettering by Jerry Thoms[on]

History of 'Old George'

'Old George' from the rear

Pumping Unit

Left View of 'Old George'

Front View of 'Old George'

Havoline Cans from U.S. and abroad

Service You Can Trust

Erol and Susan's Fillin' Station

A few years ago Vernon Walker from Tennessee was reading *Check the Oil*, a publication for collectors, when he noticed an ad for the sale of a NOS (in box) Texaco service station and trailer. It sounded interesting and Vernon didn't mind having a miniature service station (he didn't know what the trailer had to do with the service station), so he called to find out more.

The ad was placed in *Check the Oil* by a representative of the owner of the station. He found out that the owner was a Texaco distributor in Missouri. Vernon was given the name and address of the distributor; he gave him a call.

Vernon found out the reason the owner was offering a trailer with the service station…it was a REAL, honest-to-goodness Texaco station that had been stored in a trailer. Out of curiosity, he decided to drive to Missouri and visit the distributor. To his surprise, every piece of the prefabricated station was there, along with the instructions for installation.

Vernon was a little nervous about telling his wife that he had just purchased a Texaco station…doesn't *everyone* have a full-size, fully-equipped service station in their backyard?

Vernon hired a contractor to assemble the station. Although the instructions accompanied the station, challenges did arise during the assembly. The builder of the station was contacted so that some light could be shed on exactly where a few of the pieces fit. The builder of the station, located in New Orleans, had discarded the plans for that particular station; but, as luck would have it, a long-time employee of the builder was able to assist. Photographs of the pieces in question were sent to New Orleans. From the photos the employee was able to assist Vernon with the erection of the station.

The only part of the station and its contents that is not original is the 1950 flip post rack that Vernon had to install. You see, Vernon uses the rack in his service station to work on his other hobby…show cars. The original rack would not fit his cars.

Thank you, Vernon, for preserving a piece of our past…a big piece of our past.

MISCELLANEOUS

Hand-painted, tin, No Pricing Available

One-sided, key hole, door sign
(distributor), $375-500

"Wherever You Go", painted tin, $60-90

One-sided, key hole, door sign (agent),
$375-500

Filling Station, 42" porcelain (note:
block letter style), $1500-1800

Lubrication Chart, 1932-1937, $35-40

Filling Station, 42" porcelain (note: script letter style), $1500-1800

Filling Station Sign with Price Sign (26 x 18), two-sided, painted tin, extremely rare, No Pricing Available

'Safety First' Lost-Time Injury, $1450-1800

"Buy The Best", embossed tin, $525-600

'Easy Pour Can' porcelain sign, $1400-1900

Petrole Crystalite, painted tin, $475-600; Hat, $145-175;
Havoline 'F', painted tin, $275-350

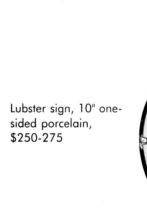

Lubster sign, 10" one-
sided porcelain,
$250-275

Marfak Grease No. 2, brass, $20-25;
Gasoline Shipping Tag, $8-10

Marfak Lubrication sign, $950-1000
(for all)

Aviation Products, 24" porcelain, $2400-2800

Lubster sign, 15" one-sided porcelain, $325-400

No Smoking, porcelain, $1400-1600

Gas Pump Plate, 8" one-sided porcelain, $200-275

Drain and Refill curb sign, two-sided porcelain, $500-675

Lubster sign, 8" one-sided porcelain, $200-275

'Notice' from The Texas Company, $150-225

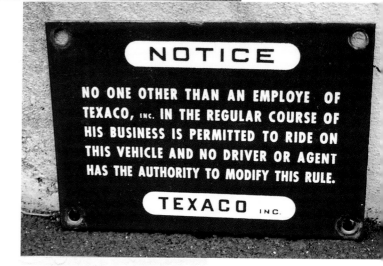

'Notice' from Texaco Inc., $150-225

Sky Chief curb sign, two-sided painted metal, $1200-1600

Pump Plate, 15" curved porcelain, $300-375

'Notice' from The Texas Company, $150-225

'Notice' from The Texas Pipeline Company, $150-225

'Clean, Clear, Golden,' one-sided porcelain, 14 x 12, dated 1931, $500-625

'Clean, Clear, Golden,' one-sided porcelain, 16 x 15.5, dated 1930, $500-625

'Clean, Clear, Golden,' 10" curved pump plate, $875-950

'Clean, Clear, Golden,' flanged porcelain, $875-1000

'Clean, Clear, Golden,' 15" curved pump plate, $675-775

'Clean, Clear, Golden, Crankcase Service,' one-sided
porcelain, $800-950

'Clean, Clear, Golden,' flanged
porcelain, $425-500

Stays Full *Longer*, small one-sided porcelain, $700-900

Stays *Full* Longer, painted tin (1930s), $550-600

Fire Chief, one-sided painted tin, $100-125

No Smoking, The Texas Company, one-sided porcelain,
$180-240

Texaco Motor Oil, Ford, one-sided porcelain, $400-550

Texaco Motor oil, flanged porcelain
(1920s), $750-900

Texaco Location Map, painted tin, $275-300; (signs on right,
one-sided painted tin, $100-125 each)

Porcelain letters for tanker truck, $125-160

Identification tags for oil grades, two-sided porcelain, $75-100 each

Private Road warning, embossed metal, $75-100

No Smoking warning sign, one-sided embossed tin, $550-675

Lubster attachment with porcelain sign, $850-1000

Lubster sign, porcelain, $475-550

Texaco Lubrication Service, one-sided porcelain, $550-675

Texas Pipeline 'Caution' porcelain sign, $225-300

Lubster attachment with porcelain sign
(larger version), $850-1000

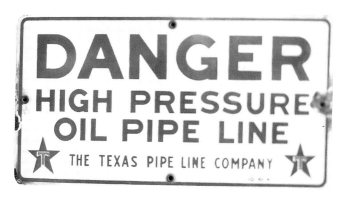

Texas Pipeline 'Danger' porcelain sign,
$225-300

Texaco/Ethyl curb sign, two-sided
porcelain, $675-800

Brass Motor Oil Tags, $25-30 each

Industrial Lubricants,
embossed painted tin,
$75-125

Certified Lubrication, one-sided porcelain, 1932, $325-400

Oil-Change Reminder, one-sided
cardboard, $70-110

Large, one-sided porcelain, 1940s, $550-675

Small, one-sided porcelain, 1939, $675-750

Farm Lubricants, one-sided porcelain, 1950s, $475-600

'Certified' Service, tombstone sign, two-sided, porcelain, 1920s, $450-800

'Certified' Service curb sign, two-sided porcelain, $375-450

'Registered' Rest Room curb sign, two-sided painted metal, $90-110

'Tower of Power' window display, cardboard, $90-110

'New' Motor Oil, two-sided painted tin, $225-375

'Localized For You' painted tin, $175-225

'Tower of Power' pump plate, plastic, $100-125

'Quality Line' Products, two-sided painted tin, $90-110

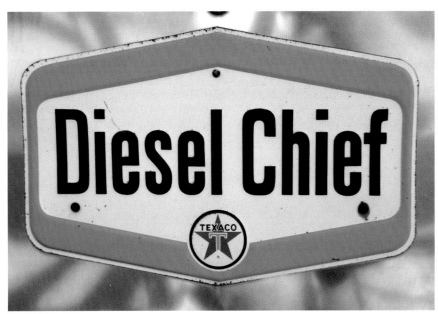

Diesel Chief pump plate, embossed tin, $275-325

Sky Chief Petrox pump plate, 8 x 14 porcelain, $175-225

Fire-Chief pump plate, 8 x 12 porcelain, $175-225

Sky Chief pump plate, 8 x 12 porcelain, $225-275

Diesel Chief pump plate, porcelain,
$180-275

Diesel Chief 'L' pump plate, porcelain,
$180-275

Diesel Fuel '2' pump plate, porcelain,
$200-325

Fuel Chief '1' pump plate, porcelain,
$1200-1500

Sky Chief pump plate, 12 x 18 porcelain, $100-125

Sky Chief curved pump plate, 8 x 12 porcelain, $140-200

Fire-Chief curved pump plate, 8 x 12 porcelain, $125-150

Sky Chief Petrox (green) pump plate, 12 x 18 porcelain, $100-125

Fire-Chief pump plate, 12 x 18 porcelain, $100-125

Fire-Chief pump plate, curved, 12 x 18 porcelain, $110-125

Home Lubricant display with cans
(cardboard), $275-300

No Smoking, 1960/70s, one-sided porcelain, $175-250

'Insulated' Motor Oil, curb sign, two-
sided (painted metal, 1938), $450-525

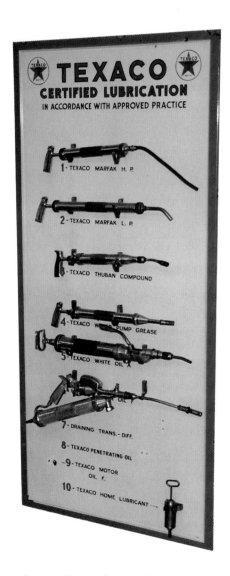

Grease-Gun rack, porcelain, 1934,
$1000-1400

Motor Oil sign, one-sided porcelain (26", rare), No Pricing Available

Motor Oil sign, two-sided porcelain (42", 1932), $725-800

Industrial Lubricants, one-sided, painted tin, $100-135

Motor Oil sign, two-sided porcelain (20", rare), No Pricing Available

Marfak *Lubrication*, one-sided, painted metal, $350-400

Clear burning Kerosene, one-sided, painted tin, $100-125

Early electric one-sided sign, rare (thought to be one-of-a-kind), No Pricing Available

Texacare electric one-sided sign (plastic), $200-300

Insulated Motor Oil, die-cut, one-sided porcelain (22.5 x 36.5, 1940), $525-600

One-sided, porcelain, 36" x 28", $225-300

Certified Lubrication, one-sided porcelain, $325-400

Long-spout lubricant on top of lubricant container, $100-150 each

Home Lubricant, 1930s, $30-45

Home Lubricant, 1950s, $35-45

Early green, 'Upper Lubricant' containers, rare, $60-80 each

Railroad 'Hot Box Coolant' (1940/50s), $35-50

Railroad 'Hot Box Coolant' (1960/70s), $35-50

Texwax paraffine (1920/30s), $60-75

'Made In Texas' pin back, 1908, $325-475

Texwax paraffine (1940/50s), $30-40

Small pin back, 1914, $175-250

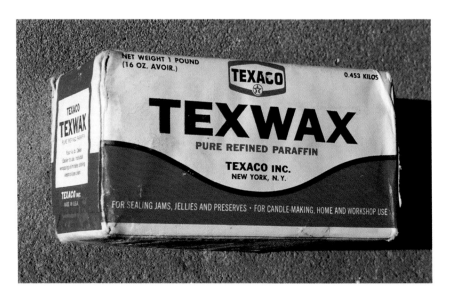

Texwax paraffin (they finally spelled it correctly) (1960/70s), $20-25

Lamp, 75th anniversary, $150-200

Scottie-dog lamp, $475-550; 75th anniversary lamp shade, $150-175

Scottie-dog window decal (early 1930s), $40-50

Scottie-dog pin back, $125-160

Scottie-dog, die-cut advertising piece (1932), No Pricing Available

Window decals from 1930s, $40-50 each

Scottie-dog fan, 1932, rare, $140-180 each

Scottie-dog pin back, $140-180

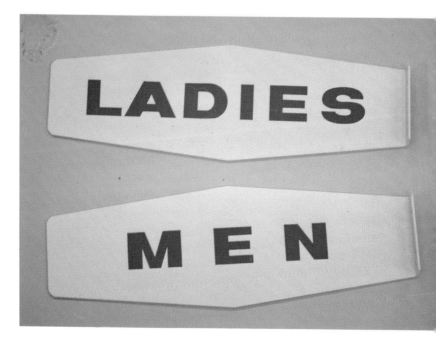

'Ladies' 'Men' Rest Room signs, 1960s, $50-60 each

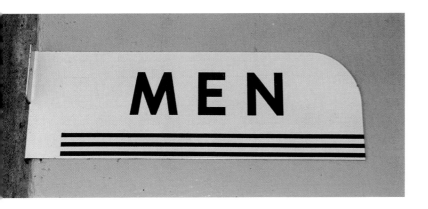

'Men' Rest Room sign, 1940/50s, $60-70

'Ladies' Rest Room sign, 1940/50s, $60-70

Rest Room customer pledge, 1930s,
$125-150

Rest Room customer pledge, 1958,
$40-60

Rest Room Keys, 1940/
50s, $140-160 set

Rest Room Keys, $60-90 set

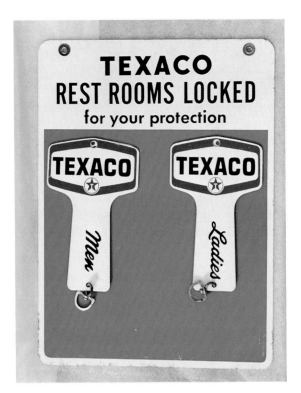

Brass Lock (The Texas Company), $90-110

Brass Lock, $65-80

Rest Room Keys, 1950/60s, $125-150 set

Brass Lock, $140-150

Brass Lock, $70-95

Early Curb-Side Pump (made exclusively for Texaco), $300-350

Miles-per-Gallon Slide, $15-20

Fire Extinguisher, $175-200

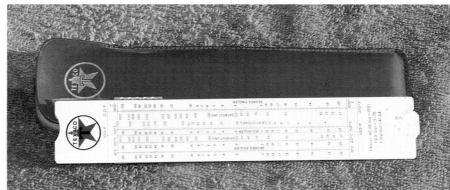

Slide Rule, $100-175

Patches, $8-15 each

Oil-Filter Radio (NOS), $40-55

Sampler Oil Bottles, $150-175

Anti-Freeze Tester,
$90-125

Sampler Oil Bottles, $175-225

Auto Window
Hanger for
clothes, $15-20

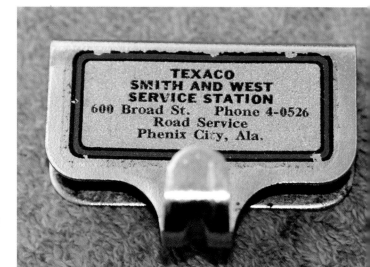

Oil Change Tag, $10-15

Safety Match Cover, $140-160

Money Clip, $35-40

Money Clip, $175-200

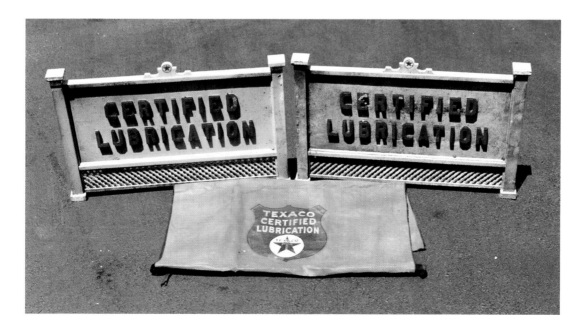

Salesman's Sample Kit, $475-600

Salesman's Sample Kit, $1500-2000

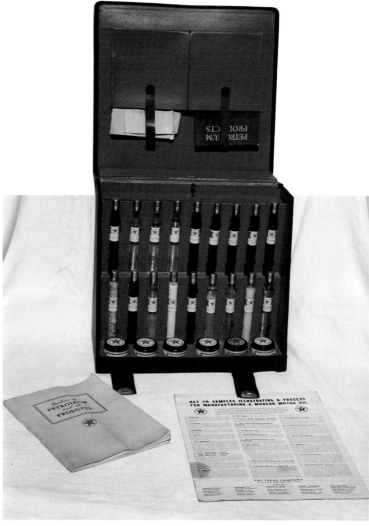

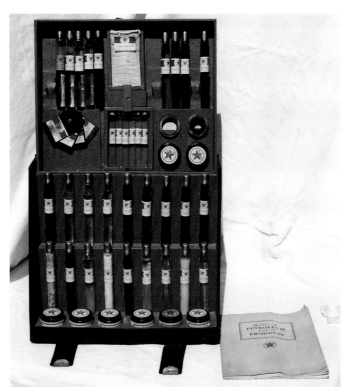

(inside of salesman's kit, showing
product samples)

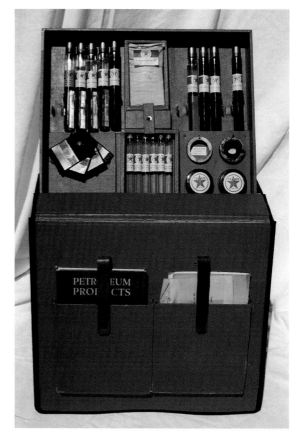

Insulated Motor Cycle Oil, $75-100

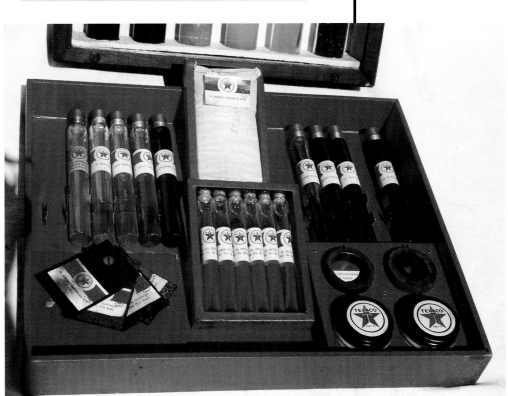

Wooden Stilts, $100-125

TEXACO
BATTERY SERVICE

Battery Service, one-sided porcelain, $275-400

NOTICE

GAMBLING PROHIBITED ON THESE PREMISES

TEXACO INC.

'NOTICE', one-sided porcelain, Gambling Prohibited, No Pricing Available

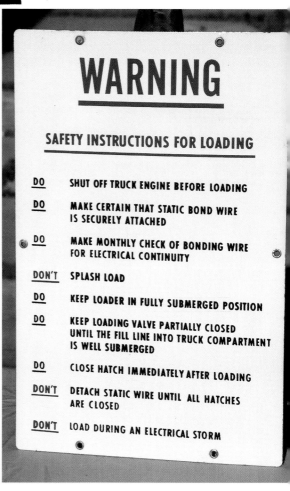

WARNING

SAFETY INSTRUCTIONS FOR LOADING

DO	SHUT OFF TRUCK ENGINE BEFORE LOADING
DO	MAKE CERTAIN THAT STATIC BOND WIRE IS SECURELY ATTACHED
DO	MAKE MONTHLY CHECK OF BONDING WIRE FOR ELECTRICAL CONTINUITY
DON'T	SPLASH LOAD
DO	KEEP LOADER IN FULLY SUBMERGED POSITION
DO	KEEP LOADING VALVE PARTIALLY CLOSED UNTIL THE FILL LINE INTO TRUCK COMPARTMENT IS WELL SUBMERGED
DO	CLOSE HATCH IMMEDIATELY AFTER LOADING
DON'T	DETACH STATIC WIRE UNTIL ALL HATCHES ARE CLOSED
DON'T	LOAD DURING AN ELECTRICAL STORM

'WARNING', one-sided porcelain, $125-200

TEXACO

NOTICE

No illegal drugs, intoxicating beverages, firearms or weapons allowed on this property.

Persons under the influence of drugs or alcohol not allowed on this property.

All persons, vehicles and other personal effects entering or leaving this property subject to search.

'NOTICE', one-sided porcelain, $300-350

'The Texas Company', one-sided porcelain, 1938, $225-350

Deck of Playing Cards (red), $60-85

Double Deck of Playing Cards (green), $60-85

Coat or Shirt Button, $35-40

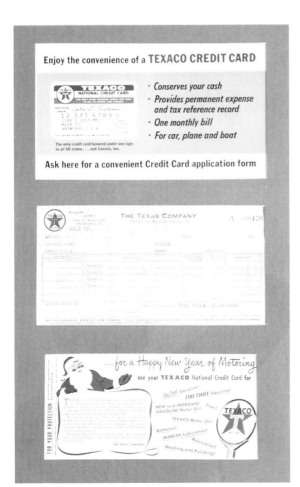

Hat Button, $35-45

Framed Credit-Card Advertisement,
$50-60

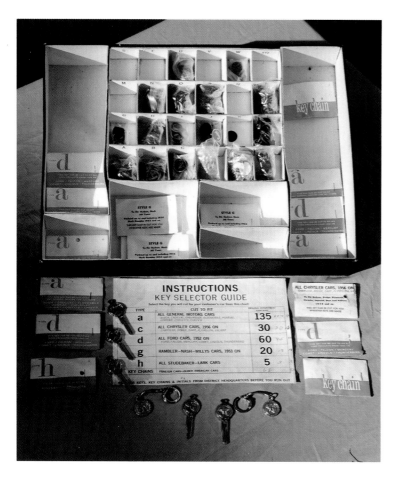

Kit for making Texaco Keys with Key Chains, $225-250 (for complete kit)

Ship's Compass, $300-350

Radiator Cleaner (cone-shaped, waxed cardboard), $100-150

Farm Products Scale, $550-600

Super Chief Battery (NOS), $100-125

Marfak Caps (NOS), $40-60

Battery Radio (NOS in box), $45-55

Spark Plug, $15-20

Mirror, $70-90

57

Sun-Visor Mirror, $90-120

Oil Dispenser Identification, early, $90-110

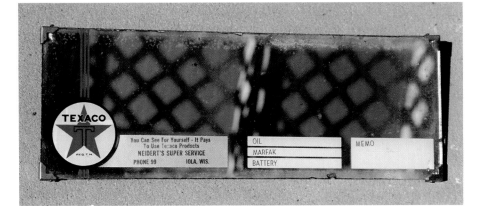

Sun-Visor Mirror, $110-125

Watch Fob with Leather Strap, $225-275

TexWax Advertisement, No Pricing Available

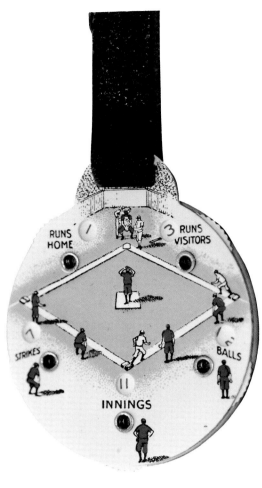

Watch Fob (early) with Gold Chain,
$225-275

Watch Fob, celluloid, $475-550

(reverse side keeps baseball scoring)

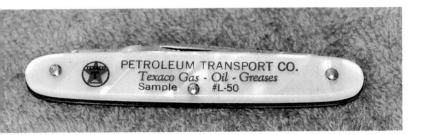

Pocket Knife, $100-125

Pocket Knife, $110-130

Pocket Knife, $120-155

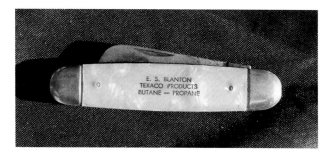

Pocket Knife, $40-45

Pocket Knife, $75-100

Multi-purpose Knife, $75-100; with Fire-Hat Key Chain, $15-20

Retractable Ruler with porcelain logo, $80-95

Magnet Clip, $40-45

60

Cigarette Lighter,
engraved, $70-85

Cigarette Lighter with porcelain logo,
$125-135

Cigarette Lighter with plastic inset,
$90-110

Cigarette Lighter with painted logo,
$70-85

Cigar and Pipe Lighter, $140-160

Cigarette Lighter with porcelain logo,
$125-160

Bottle Lighter, $40-55

Cigarette Lighter (NOS), $70-90

Cigarette Lighter (front of lighter),
$40-60

Cigarette Lighter, small, $40-60

(reverse side of lighter)

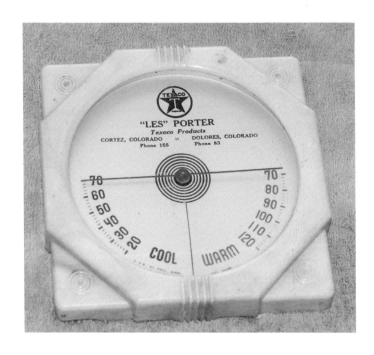

Bake-Lite Thermometer, $160-180

Thermometer, small, $75-90

62

Thermometer, $80-110

Left:
Thermometer,
$120-160

Above:
Thermometer,
$100-125

Thermo-Scope (very hard to find), $90-110

Right:
Thermometer and
Clock, $125-140

Thermometer, $100-125

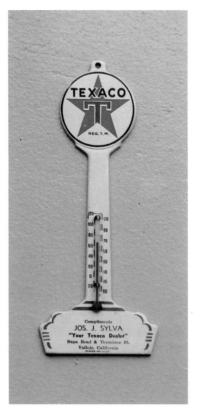

Key Chain, 1953, $25-35

Thermometer, plastic, $90-100

Thermometer, metal, $90-110

Key Chain, Scottie Dogs, $35-50

Key Chain, $45-60

Key Chain, $30-45

Key Chain, $35-45

Key Chain, $30-40

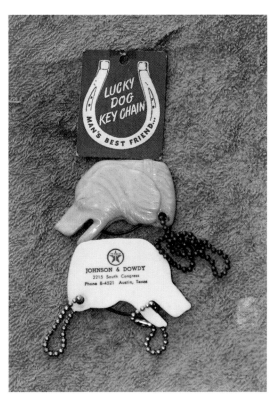

Lucky Dog Key Chain, Dog-shaped Key Chain (front and back is shown), $45-60 each

Key Chain, $20-25

Key Chain, $30-40

Combination Key Chain and Ruler, $50-65

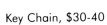

Gold-colored Key, $20-25

Plate, 1978, $40-65

Christmas Salt and Pepper in box (NOS), $50-70

Plate, 1911 (Inscription: Fire At The Texas Co's Dock and Warehouse), No Pricing Available

Dish Towel, $75-95

Salt Bags, $20-30 each

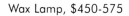
Wax Lamp, $450-575

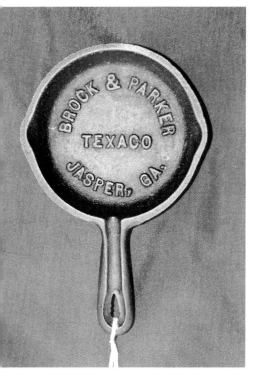
Fry Pan, rare, $100-125

Close-up for Inscription

Pin Back, $75-125

Pin Back, $25-30

Pin Back, $75-125

Pin Back (1920s), $140-160

Pin Back, aviation, $30-40

Texaco Motor Oil Wrench, $100-125

Alarm Clock, $250-300

(reverse side: Texaco Gasoline)

Wall Clock, large, $225-250

Alarm Clock, $250-300

Playing Cards, $75-100

Gas Gage Ruler, $60-80 each

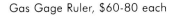

Post Card, Wyoming, early, $8-10

Post Card, San Antonio, early, $10-15

Post Card, Montana, early, $8-10

Oil Bottle, embossed,
Imperial quart, $150-175

Oil Bottle, embossed, .5
Imperial quart, $150-175

Cup Grease shipping box, wooden,
$75-125

Fat-Boy Banks (note difference in color), $125-150

Clear, Clean, Full-Bodied shipping box,
wooden, $120-140

License Plate Attachment, $100-150

70

License Plate Attachment, $175-200

License Plate Attachment, $225-250

Oil Rack, $20-30; Aviation Cans, $15-20 each; Havoline Cans, $10-15 each

Quality Line Products (Rack), $150-175; (Cans), $15-20 each

Super Motor Detergent Dispenser, $150-175

Oil Rack, $20-30; Oil Cans, $10-15 each

Leaded Glass Window, $1200-1600

Oil Rack with Sign, $375-450; Oil Cans, top row, $20-25 each; Aviation Cans, center row, $55-85; Oil Cans, bottom row (right and left cans), $30-35 each; Oil Can, bottom row (center can), $60-40

Motor Oil Change Reminder, $20-25

Oil Lubster in wheels, $1800-2500 (restored value)

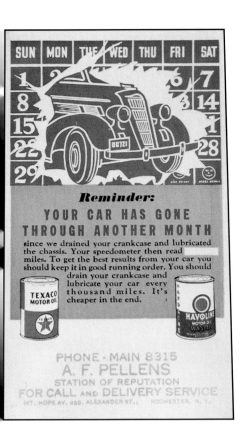

Motor Oil Change Reminder, $20-25

Motor Oil Change Reminder, $20-25

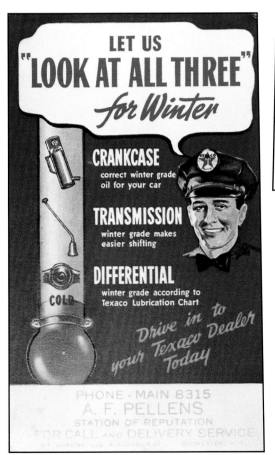

Battery and Tire Check-up Reminder,
$20-25

Winter Check-up Reminder, $20-25

Fuel Chief Heating Oil Mailer, $20-25

Metal Cabinet with Texaco logo for cabinet handles, $100-125

Whiskey Flask, $175-225

Fuel Chief Heating Oil Sign (die-cut masonite), $250-300

APPAREL AND ACCESSORIES

Brief Case, $450-525

Green Cover-all, $100-125

Summer Station Hat, $125-140

Station Hat and Bow-tie, $125-165

Winter Station Hat, $145-175

Green Cover-all (front and back view), $100-125

Foreman's Club Lapel Pin, $65-85

Security Guard Badge, $100-125

Fire Chief Shirt, $600-800

Texaco Jacket with Badges, No Pricing Available

Fire Chief Baseball Uniform, $375-450

Baseball Uniform, early, $380-475

Name Badge, brass with porcelain logo, $350-450

Name Badge, porcelain, $325-475

Lapel Pin, $20-30

Earrings, $60-80

ASH TRAYS

Sheppard's Texaco Station, Lancaster, Ohio, $30-40

Ben A. Parkinson, $40-50

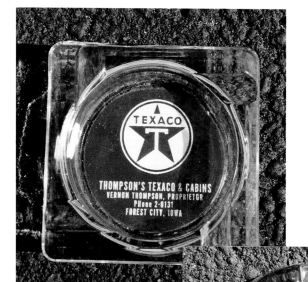

Thompson's Texaco and Cabins, Forest City, Iowa, $35-55

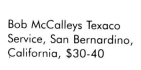

Bob McCalleys Texaco Service, San Bernardino, California, $30-40

Crosby/Whipple Oil Company (ash tray with thermometer), Lockport, Illinois, $80-90

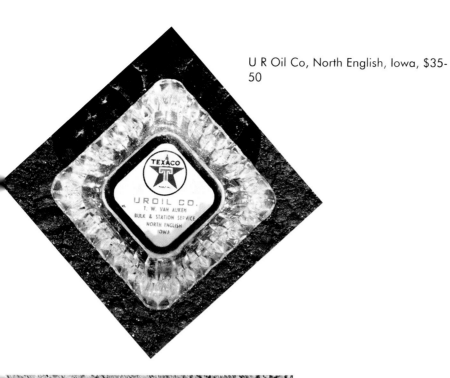

U R Oil Co, North English, Iowa, $35-50

Gene Hillger, Alpine, Texas, $40-55

Jess L. Dale, McKinney, Texas, $40-55

Charlie's Texaco, Cedar Grove, Indiana, $40-60

Ansel Strommen, Brodhead Motor
Service, $40-60

Brass Ash Tray with porcelain logo, $110-140

Roy E. Gourley, Lebanon, Missouri, $75-90

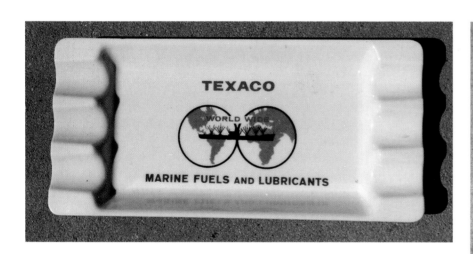

Texaco Marine Fuels and Lubricants, $60-80

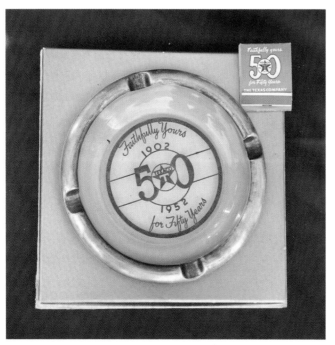

Faithfully Yours for Fifty Years (note: book of matches in corner of ash tray), $140-160

The Star Shines On (depicts logos from 1903 to 1981), $75-100

AVIATION PRODUCTS

Airplane Oil, one quart, (from 1930s) extremely rare, $850-1000

Aviation Fuels and Lubricants, painted tin, very rare (from early 1940s), $750-1000

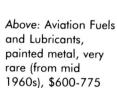

Aircraft Engine Oil, one quart (from 1940s), $85-110

Above: Aviation Fuels and Lubricants, painted metal, very rare (from mid 1960s), $600-775

Right: StarJet-5 Synthetic Turbine Oil, one quart (from 1960s), $50-60

Center: Aircraft Engine Oil, one gallon, $80-90

Far right: Aircraft Engine Oil, one quart, 50s logo with delta, $20-30

Ethyl Aviation Gasoline, wooden crate, $110-135

Pilot's Log Book (from 1920s/1930s), $130-145

Pilot's Log Book (from 1940s/1950s), $130-145

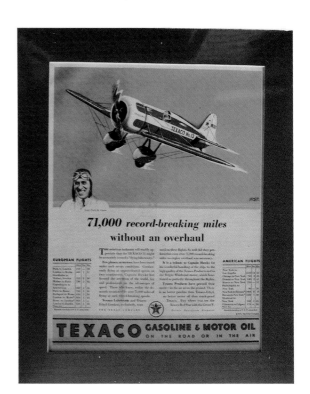

'71,000 Record-Breaking Miles', #13
Airplane, $100-125

Texaco 'Aviation' nail clippers, $25-35

'Making Air History', #5 Airplane, History-making flight
(1929), $100-125

AWARDS

Top left: Dealer Training award, 1940, $40-55

Center left: Certificate of Merit, 1942, $60-75

Bottom left: 20-year Service award, 1953 (award to: Mr. Kutzer), $50-75

Top right: Salesmanship award, 1953, $55-65

Bottom right: 20-year Dealer award, 1954 (award to: Mrs. Kutzer), $75-100

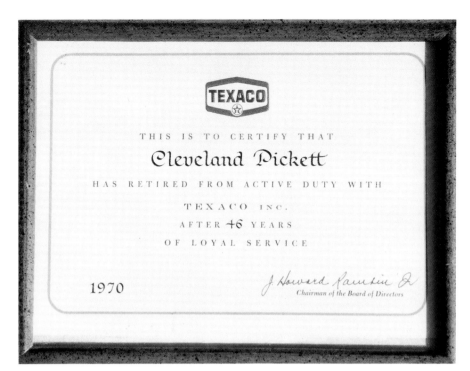

46-year Retirement award, $60-70

Service Plaque,
1947, $70-90

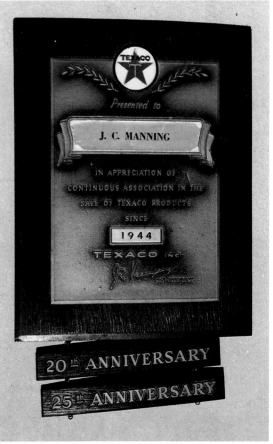

Service Plaque, 1939, $75-95

Service Plaque, 1947, $70-90

Service Plaque, 1944, $70-90

Service Plaque, 1952, $70-80

Service Plaque, 1956, $65-75

Texaco Sponsored Track and Field, 1973, $50-70

(reverse side of medal)

Service Plaque, 1957, $60-70

Far left: Texaco Sponsored Track and Field, 1974, $50-70

Left: (reverse side of medal)

Right: Texaco Sponsored Track and Field, $50-70

Far right: (reverse side of medal)

Far left: Texaco Sponsored Track and Field, 1976, $50-70

Left: (reverse side of medal)

Texaco Sponsored Track and Field, 1977, $50-70

(reverse side of medal)

Ship's Wheel Award (cigarette lighter), $475-525

Texaco Sponsored Track and Field, 1977 (silver), $50-70

(reverse side of medal)

Sales Award, 1959 (Trinidad), $200-250

Safety Award (watch fob), $125-170

Safety Award (key chain), $75-100

Honor Station Award, brass, $375-450

Wooden, Laser-cut Award, $250-300

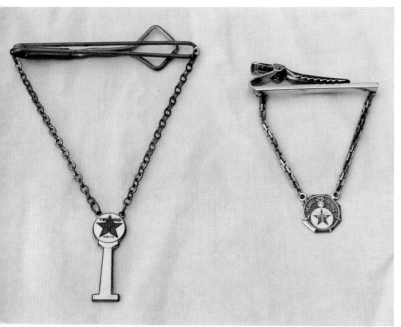

Tie Clip, left, $65-75; Tie Clip, right, $110-140

Safe Driver Lapel Pin, one year award, $35-55

Safe Driver Awards, 1, 2, 3, 4 year, $40-60 each

Safety Award, million man hours, $120-145

Safe Driver Lapel Pins, 1, 2 year awards, $40-50 each

Safe Driver Awards Display, $40-60 each

(close-up of pin to show detail)

Service Award, watch band, $100-150

Service Award, lapel pin,
$70-90

Service Award Charm, $70-90

Service Award (20 years) tie clasp, $80-100

Service Award (25 years) tie
clasp, $90-110

Service Award (20 years) tie
clasp,$90-110

Service Award (25 years) ring,
$550-600

Service Award (25 years) ring,
$550-600

Appreciation Award (20
years) lapel pin, $95-110

Service Award (25 years)
lapel pin, $95-110

Safety Award (2 years)
lapel pin, early, $110-120

Service Award (20 years) lapel pin,
$95-110

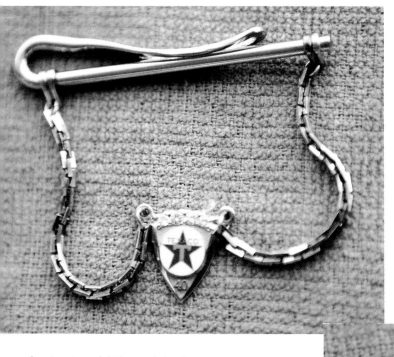

Service Award (40 years) tie clasp,
$150-175

Safety Award (5 years) lapel pin, early,
$110-120

Sales Award (1 year) lapel pin, very
early, $125-150

91

Service Award tie clasp, $80-100

Service Award tie clasp, $80-100

Service Award tie clasp, $80-100

Service Award tie clasp, $60-80

Service Award tie clasp, $90-100

1936 Fire Chief, lapel pin, No Pricing Available

Service Award tie clasp, $120-140

92

BANNERS & FLAGS

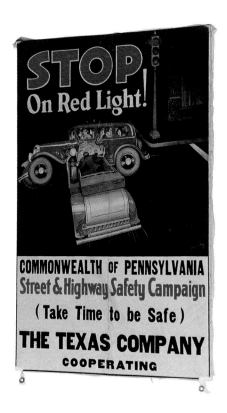

'DIM your lights' safety campaign (painting on canvas), No Pricing Available

'STOP on red light' safety campaign (painting on canvas), No Pricing Available

Goodrich tires (painting on canvas), $275-375

Gasoline and motor oil book marker, very early, $75-90

Jumbo the elephant, radio show with Jimmy Durante, $275-300

'Christmas Greetings' coupon book, window display,
$150-275

'608 gallons please!' buy wisely, window display (early),
$100-150

EASY POUR 2 qt. can, very nice early poster, $200-275

The NEW and
Better, Texaco
(banner), $145-
175

Chek-Chart window display, 'Not a squeak in a thousand miles', $200-250

New Golden Motor Oil, get acquainted offer N.O.S. banner, $140-225

Motor Lubrication Guide, 'The right grade for your needs', $175-250

'Texaco is like an open book', Saturday Evening Post, Feb. 1926, $95-150

Texaco Motor Oil Banner, 1935, $90-120

Top right: Texaco Chemical Company (newer flag), $70-90

First center right: Texaco Starport Flag (newer flag), $65-85

Second center right: Corley Range Friendly Service, cardboard window advertising, $75-125

Bottom right: Texaco Star Bulk Plant Flag, logo used from early 1940s to 1963, $75-100

Texaco Winter Sports Special, 1972 banner, $80-125

"2 Fine Toys", $155-180

Guaranteed Protection PT anti-freeze, late 40s-early 50s,
$190-275

New Fire-Chief Gasoline, early 1930s, $175-200

Stop for a spring check up, 40s-50s banner, $125-175

"A Greater Fire-Chief", $130-150

Fall Check-up, 1950s, $130-155

Trinidad Texaco Banner, $120-135

CALTEX

38" one-sided, porcelain, $350-450

36" one-sided, porcelain, $575-700

One-sided, porcelain (very rare sign with boy displaying Caltex products—note the Havoline logo on cans), No Price Available Photo courtesy of 'Gas Station' Edizioni Modernariato Gallery, Milano

One-sided, porcelain, Five-Star Motor Oil, $450-600

"Best For Your Money", Premium Motor Oil, $425-550

One-sided, porcelain, Kerosene, $275-375

Three-year "Safe Driver" pin from Indonesia, $70-95

Two-sided, porcelain displayed in ornate wall bracket, $525-675

Small desk cigarette lighter, $80-95

4" Paper Weight, $60-75

Small give-a-way key chain (plastic),
$20-30

One-gallon Multi-Purpose Oil, $90-115

One-quart Five-Star Motor
Oil, $75-110

Marine China custard bowl, No Price Available

Marine China saucer, $80-130

Half-gallon Motor
Oil (Possibly
Arabic), $75-100

Caltex cup and saucer, $100-130

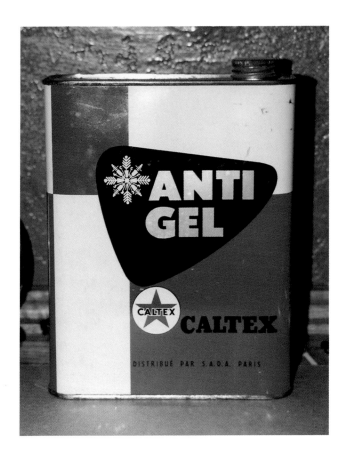

Half-gallon Extra Heavy Duty "RPM",
$75-100

Half-gallon Anti-Gel, $80-115

One-quart Five-Star "RPM", $80-100

Quart, Multigrade Supreme Motor Oil,
$80-110

Quart, Premium Extra
Heavy Duty Motor Oil,
$80-110

Quart Multigrade Havoline, $75-100

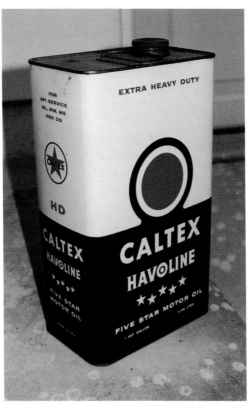

Half-gallon Extra Heavy Duty Motor Oil, $70-95

Motorway Map of Okinawa, $45-60

Petroleum Products Advertisement (notice speed limit), $45-70

Post-Card (foreign), $15-20

Pressed Tin Toy, $120-145

2.5" Pin Back, $35-50

One-sided Lubster sign, 8", $300-350

Piston Oil
Canister, $30-45

Heavy Duty Havoline, one-sided
porcelain, $800-950

1 pint Motor Oil Bottles, $100-130 each

Three-piece Glass Globe, $650-850

Small painted tin
Signs, $40-50 each

CREDIT CARDS AND IDENTIFICATION

Credit Card, paper, 1955, $110-120

Travel Card, plastic, $15-20

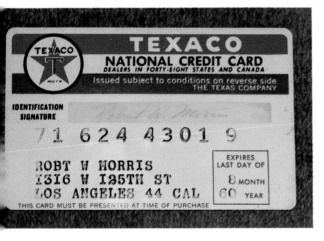

Credit Card, plastic, 1960, $20-25

Credit Card, paper, 1953, $110-120

Sample Travel Card, plastic, $25-35

Credit Card, paper, 1956, with ink blotter, $130-145

Credit Card, paper, 1954, $110-120

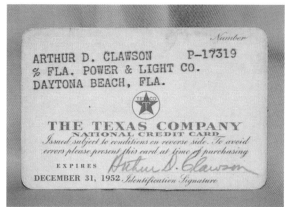

Credit Card, paper, 1952, $120-130

Credit Card, paper,
1946, $120-130

Credit Card,
paper, 1942 with
original coupons
attached, $140-
160

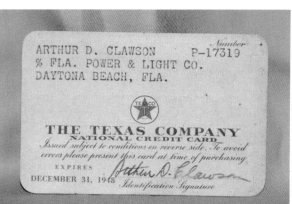

(reverse side of 1946 Credit Card)

Credit Card,
paper, 1948,
$120-130

Credit Card, 1950, paper, $120-130

Credit Card, paper, 1947, with blotter,
$130-140

Credit Card, 1951, paper, with ink
blotter, $125-145

Credit Card, paper, 1941
with original coupons
attached, $140-160

(reverse side of 1941
Credit Card)

Credit Card, paper, 1940 with original coupons attached, $140-150

Credit Card, paper, 1938, $150-175

Credit Card, paper, 1939, $150-175

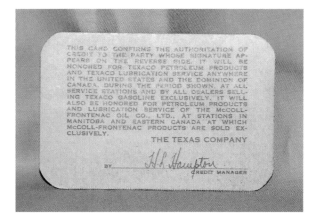

(reverse side of 1938 Credit Card)

(reverse side of 1939 Credit Card)

First-Aid Identification Certificate, $40-60

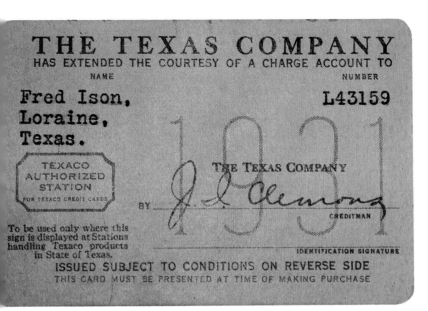

Employ Identification, $40-50

Credit Card, paper, 1931 (issued for state of Texas only), $250-300

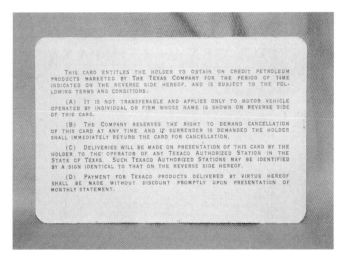

(reserve side of 1931 Credit Card)

Retirement Certificate (39 years of service to Texaco), $30-40

Driving Permit on plant property (issued 1945), $30-40

Employ Identification (1950s), $40-50

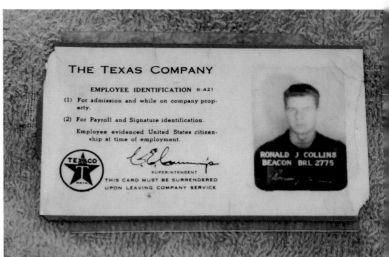

Security Guard Badge (from Lockport Works), $75-90

Identification Badge (from Lawrenceville), $60-70

Identification Badge (from Lockport Works), $60-70

DESK ACCESSORIES

Ink Blotters

'One Sign To Look For', early blotter, $60-70

'A Good Pointer', $45-55

'The Tourist's Companion', Easy-Pour Can, $50-60

World War One 'Dear Sam', early blotter, $65-75

'Economical Clean Convenient' (buy it by the bulk), $75-90

'Clean Hitting Brings In The Runs', $75-85

'Motor Oil is What Refining Makes It', $60-70

Touring with Texaco, $90-110

'A Friend To All Motorists', $60-75

Sold on Texaco Motor Oil, $50-65

'Drain, Fill, then Listen', $55-70

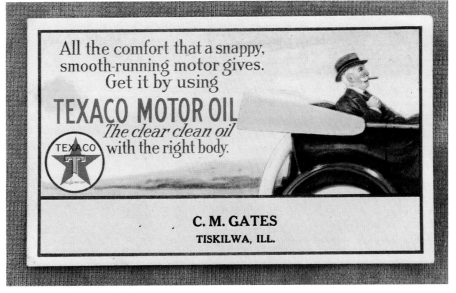

'The Clear Clean Oil with the Right Body', $70-90

'End Your Motor Troubles For Good',
$40-65

Right: 'She's In Good Shape Now' (top picture), $40-60; 'Spark Plugs Always Clean' (bottom picture), $40-60

Left: 'Steepest Hill On High' (top picture), $60-75; 'We Have The Right Grade' (center picture), $40-50; 'Goes Furthest'(bottom picture), $55-65

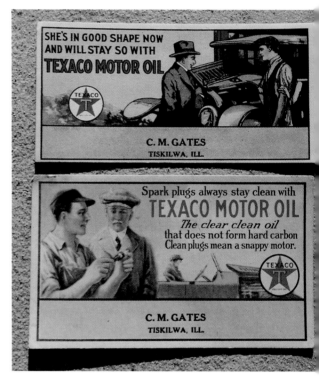

'Wise Drivers Use Texaco Motor Oil', $60-70

'Something a "Tourist" Appreciates',
Clean Rest Rooms, $30-45

Wooden Pencil, $5-10

Clip for wooden pencil, $30-40

Tape Dispenser (Marble), $40-60

Paperweight, $20-25

Paperweight, $120-145

Paperweight, $40-60

Paperweight, $70-90

Paperweight, $125-150

Stapler, $80-110

Ticket Holder, $90-110

Paper Clip, painted tin, $45-65

Mechanical Pencil, $10-15

Mechanical Pencil, $35-40

Mechanical Pencil, $35-45

Mechanical Pencil, $45-55

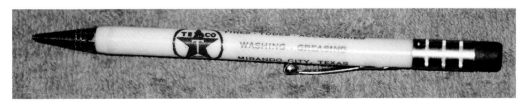

Mechanical Pencil, $35-45

Mechanical Pencil, $45-50

Mechanical Pencil, $30-35

Mechanical Pencil, $40-50

 Mechanical Pencil, $45-50

Mechanical Pencil, $10-15

 Mechanical Pencil, $45-50

Mechanical Pencil, $30-45

 Mechanical Pencil, $40-45

Mechanical Pencil, $35-40

 Wooden Pencil in container, $40-50

Mechanical Pencil, $40-45

 Mechanical Pencil, $20-25

117

EARLY GREEN CANS

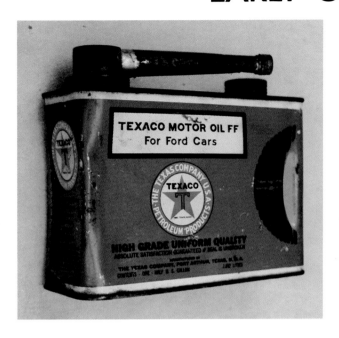

'Handy-Grip' Motor Oil for Ford Cars, $300-400

Spica Oil, 1/8 gallon, $150-175

Neatsfoot Compound,
1/2 gallon, $275-300

Hand Separator Oil, $175-250

FF Motor Oil, 5 gallon for
Ford Cars, $375-400;
Wooden Case, $90-110

Transmission Lubricant, $375-450

Motor Oil, 1/2 gallon,
$250-300

'Handy-Grip', Heavy Duty Motor Oil,
1/2 gallon, $275-300

Motor Oil, 1 pint, $110-140

'Easy Pour' Can (note: difference in
colors), $450-525 each

Thuban Compound, 5 pounds, $300-375

High Grade Grease, 1 pound,
$175-250

'Graphite' Axle Grease, small,
$200-250

'High Grade Graphite' Axle Grease, small, $200-250

'Light' Axle Grease, small, $200-250

Motor Cup Grease, 5 pound pail, $225-300

Harness Oil, 1/2 gallon, $250-300

Motor Cup Grease, 1 pound, $100-175

Motor Oil 'M' (note: wings on can), $325-400

120

Heavy Motor Oil, 1 gallon, $325-400

Motor Oil, 5 gallon, $250-325

Motor Oil, 1 gallon tall, $325-375

'Qckwork' Metal Polish, 1 quart, No Pricing Available

Light Axle Grease, 1 pound, $150-175

'Qckwork' Metal Polish, 1/2 gallon, No Pricing Available

Graphite Axle Grease, 1 pound, $140-190

Vega Axle Grease, 1 pound Army issue, $150-200

Motor Cup Grease, 25 pound pail, $125-150

Motor Cup
Grease, 1 pound,
$125-150

Chassis
Lubrication, 2
pounds, $100-
150

Liquid Wax Dressing, 1/8 gallon, $175-225

Marfax, No. 1, grease 25 lb. pail, $150-175

Marfax, No. 2, grease pail, $100-140

Marfax, No. 1, 1 pound grease can,
$100-175

Marfax, No. 0, $150-200

Liquid Wax Dressing,
1/4 gallon, $125-150

Thuban Compound 'S' (note: graphics
on side), $275-325

Extra Heavy Motor Oil, $300-350

Motor Oil, foreign, 1 liter, $75-125

'Clean, Clear, Golden', No. E, one gallon, $175-225

'Clean, Clear, Golden', No. F, one gallon, $150-175

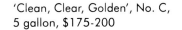

'Clean, Clear, Golden', Handy-Grip, No. E, 1/2 gallon, $275-350

'Clean, Clear, Golden', No. C, 5 gallon, $175-200

Home Lubricant (late teens/20s),
$225-275

Home Lubricant (1920s/30s),
$175-200

Home Lubricant (1930s/40s),
$150-175

Machine at Port Arthur filling Texaco Home Lubricant
containers shown in above center photo

Machine at Port Arthur assembly line, same Home Lubricant
containers as shown in above right photo

FOREIGN SIGNS

16" flanged, porcelain sign (France, 1930s), $750-875

Crystalite flanged, porcelain sign
(Africa, 1920s), No Pricing Available

Carabao Petroleum, flanged, porcelain
sign (Philippines, 1920-30s), $1400-
1800

'Oil For Autos', flanged, porcelain sign
(France, 1920-30s), $850-1000

Motor Spirit (reverse side), (Australia, 1920-30s)

Motor Oil, flanged, porcelain sign (front), $675-825

Motor Spirit and Oil, flanged, porcelain
sign (Australia, 1930s), $450-525

'Pure, Clear, Golden', two-sided porcelain sign (Germany,
1930s), $900-1150

Petroleum, tombstone-shaped, one-sided porcelain sign (Dutch, 1940-50s), $475-550

'Petrol', tombstone-shaped, one-sided porcelain sign (Germany, 1920-30s), $500-575

Texaco, Girtex, flanged, porcelain sign (1920-30s), $475-550

Motor Oil, concave, one-sided, porcelain sign (Germany, 1930-40s), $875-975

'Perfect Lubrication Leaves no Carbon', one-sided, porcelain (Australia, 1930-40s), $425-500

129

'Clean Clear' Motor Oil, one-sided,
porcelain sign (Australia, 1930-40s),
$475-600

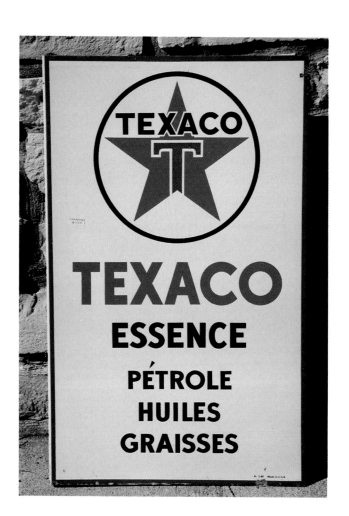

'Gas Oil Greases', flanged, porcelain
sign (France, 1940-50s), $475-550

'Gasoline and Oils' , flanged, porcelain
(Puerto Rico, 1930-40s), $475-550

'Oil For Autos',concave, one-sided, porcelain (France, 1930-
40s), $950-1200

PHOTOGRAPHS

Service Station Number 24 in Los Angeles, $200-250

Country Service Station, $140-160

Service Station from the 1920s (is that
one of Al Capone's gang?), $175-225

Delivering gasoline to Service Station, $250-275

Ultra-modern Gas Tanker from the 1930s, $200-250

Busy Station in New York, late 1930 or early 1940s, $175-200

Texaco Train in oil fields, 1926, $150-175

Texaco in Africa, $125-135

Employees with 20 years or more service, pictured on and around tank car, 1929, $200-250

Territorial and District Manager's, meeting, 1935, $175-200

Champions of Joliet Factory League,
1929, $240-260

Texaco Baseball Team from Dallas,
Texas, $250-275

133

GLOBES

Note that the black out-lined 'T' was fazed out in 1939-1943. The white out-lined 'T' was utilized thereafter. This was true in all Texaco products.

Metal-band, glass faces, 15", $1800-2200

Etched, Chimney-top, $4500-6000

Metal-band, leaded glass, 15", $3800-4500

Metal-band, milk glass faces, 15", $1800-2400

Metal-band, leaded glass, center 22", left and right 15", (photo courtesy of *Petroleum Collectibles Monthly* Archives), No Pricing Available

Texaco Star Globe, (Southeast Asia &
Australia, 1920-30s), $4000-5000

Two-sided, porcelain globe, 15" (1938), $1200-1600

Ethyl, One-piece, raised letter, $1200-1600

One-piece, etched, $1000-1200

Left: Fire-Chief
Hat, No Pricing
Available
Photo courtesy of
Mark Anderson,
Collectors Auction
Service

Right: One-piece,
raised letter,
$475-600

Three-piece, glass (black outlined 'T'), $475-550

Left: Sky Chief, three-piece,
glass (white outlined 'T'),
$475-550

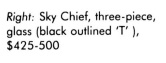

Right: Sky Chief, three-piece,
glass (black outlined 'T'),
$425-500

Diesel Chief, three-piece, glass (black outlined 'T'), $800-1000

Ethyl, three-piece, glass (black outlined 'T'), $750-900

Diesel Fuel, three-piece, glass Gill body (white outlined 'T'), $475-550

Diesel Fuel, three-piece, glass Gill body (white outlined 'T'), $475-550

Three-piece, plastic (white outlined 'T'), $100-145

137

HAVOLINE

Blue Grass Axle Grease, embossed tin, $175-225

Banner from the Boston Auto Show, 1914, $250-290

Indian Gasoline, very early (notice colors), $775-875

Indian Gas on 15" metal band, $1500-1800

(side view of Indian Globe—FYI: there was a smaller version of this globe with a 4" base)

Indian Globe, one-piece etched (front view), $5500-6200

Glass Globe, three piece (1930s), $450-475

Etched Globe, narrow body, one piece, $1850-2200

Etched Globe, wide body, one piece (late teens to early 1920s), $1600-1800

Havoline Oil Banner, $100-125

Indian Refining Oil Can, very early, $275-350

Motor Grease, 5 lb. pail, $190-260

Motor Grease, 10 lb. pail, $120-160

Motor Grease, 1 lb. (teens to 1920s), $200-275

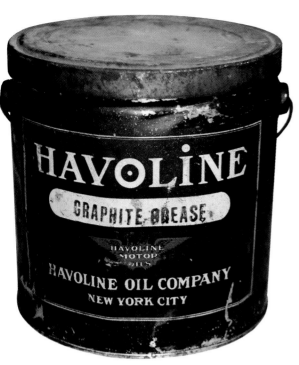

Graphite Grease, 5 lb. pail (teens to
1920s), $100-150

Oil Can, 1 gallon (teens to 1920s),
Lawrenceville, Illinois, $175-225

Oil Can, 1 gallon (teens to 1920s),
$175-225

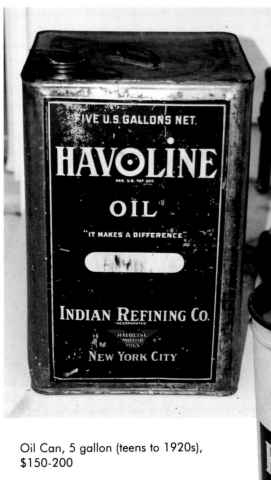

Oil Can, 5 gallon (teens to 1920s),
$150-200

Grease Can, 5 lb. (1920s), $60-90

Oil Can, 1 imperial gallon (teens to 1920s), $200-250

'The Oil For Fords', framed cardboard sign, $175-225

Porcelain Sign, early, $275-350

Reflective Sign, rare, $1000-1400

Lubster Sign, small die-cut, two-sided, painted tin, $200-275

Wooden Case, $75-120

Sign of Havoline Can, flanged, die-cut porcelain, $675-800

Two-sided Sign, porcelain, $275-325

Oil Can with Spout, $60-70

Oil Water-Transfer Decal, $25-30

Indian Gasoline Curved Sign,
porcelain (8 x 12), $275-350

Indian Gasoline Curved Sign, porcelain
(12 x 18), $300-350

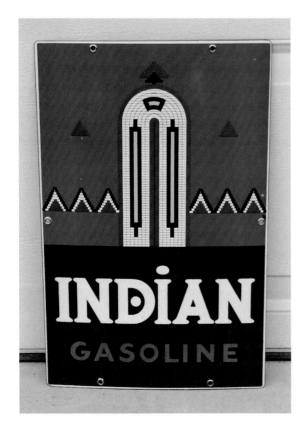

Porcelain Sign (8 x 12), $275-$350

Porcelain Sign (8 x 12), curved to fit
Visible Pump (1940s), $275-350

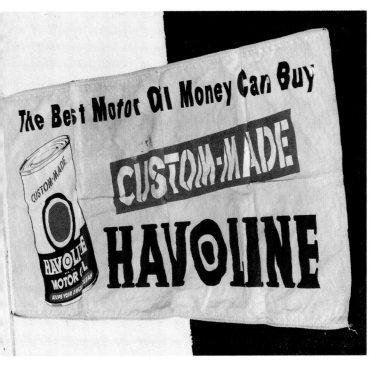

Havoline Banner, $150-175

One-sided, porcelain sign from oil rack, (teens to 1920s), $450-575

Cardboard Sign, $75-100

Porcelain Sign (1920s), $425-575

'the power oil' flanged, porcelain sign (1920s), $550-675

Painted tin, flanged sign, $400-550

Porcelain, flanged sign, $650-725

One-sided porcelain sign, $335-450

Porcelain Sign and oil rack (bottles included), $1400-1700

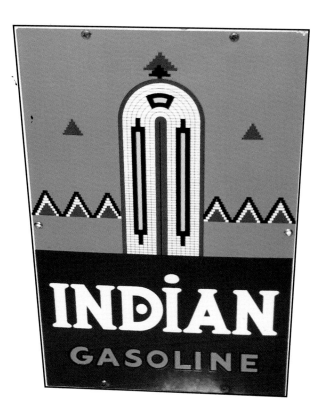

Porcelain Pump Plate sign (12 x 18), $275-325

Oil Change Reminder Tag,
$30-35

Thermometers from the 1933 World's
Fair, $85-120 each

Postcard from 1933 World's Fair,
$20-25

Havoline Truck, 1983, $100-150

Radio and box (NOS), $50-60

Oil rack without cans, $550-600

Havoline Can Display, No Pricing Available

Oil Rack without Cans, $525-575

One-sided Can, 1935 (16 x 12.5), $675-775

Later Havoline Cans Display, No Pricing Available

149

One-sided porcelain sign,
$375-450

the power oil, one-sided porcelain,
$300-475

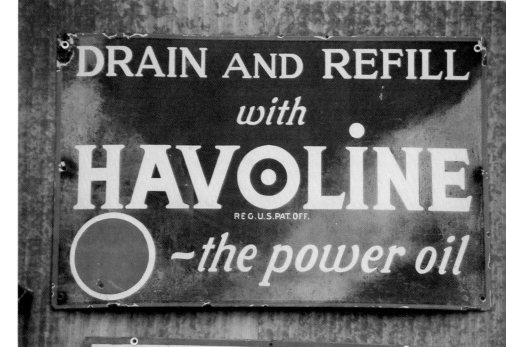

One-sided porcelain sign,
$250-375

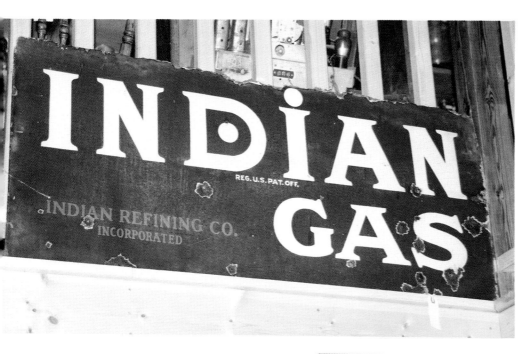

Two-sided porcelain Indian Gas, $375-475

Wood framed, painted tin sign, early, $475-575

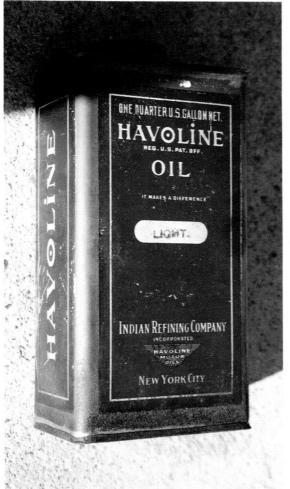

(top of can)

Havoline Sample Can (one quarter U.S. gallon), No Pricing
Available

Wayne 60 pumps, $1950-2250 (repro globes)

1 pint Motor Oil Bottles

MCCOLL-FRONTENAC

Road Guide, 1947,
Quebec and the
Maritime Provinces,
$40-55

Armour-Plate Aviation Motor Oil, advertising piece, $90-120

Road Map, Canada, $90-130

Marathon Blue,
advertising piece,
$180-190

Handy Set (note outline of Red Indian logo), No Pricing Available

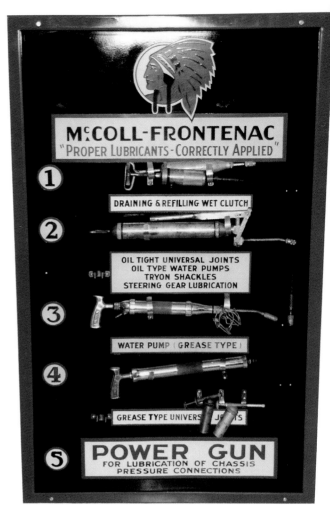

"Proper Lubricants-Correctly Applied" (porcelain power gun rack), $1800-2200

Havoline, imperial quart, $70-75

'Advanced' Havoline, imperial quart, $65-75

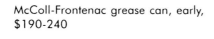

Red Indian Motor Oil, imperial gallon, $225-350

Protex All, imperial gallon anti-freeze
can, $130-160

McColl-Frontenac grease can, early,
$190-240

Red Indian Motor Oil, one pound,
$110-140

Red Indian H.P. Grease pail, $90-125

155

Red Indian Aviation, imperial quart,
$75-110

Gasoline Motor Oils, two-sided porcelain, 48", $1650-2200

Red Indian Motor Oil, imperial quart,
$70-90

Red Indian Motor Oils, one-sided porcelain, 18" x 20.5",
$775-900

Aviation Motor Oil, None Better!, one-sided porcelain,
$600-775

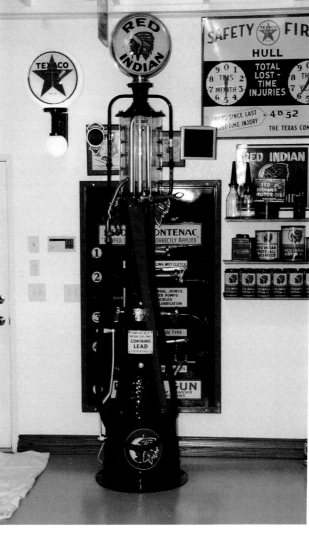

Fry pump, 5 gallon (foreground),
reproduction globe, $2400-2800

Sealed For Your Protection, one-sided porcelain, $250-325

Defense De Fumer (no smoking), $475-600

MAPS

Tour Florida, $90-110

(reverse side of map)

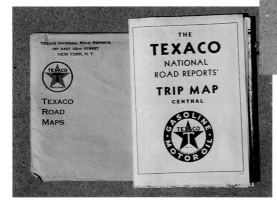

Trip Map, Central U.S., $50-60

Tour Illinois, $20-25

Tour Kansas & Nebraska, $40-50

Tour Ohio, $40-50

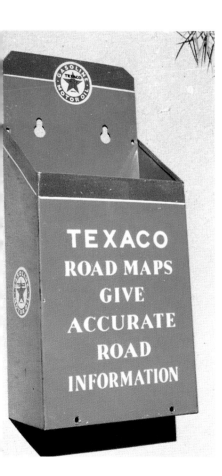

Map Holder, $175-250

Touring Service map holder, $65-80

Tour Arizona, Colorado, New Mexico, Utah, and Kansas, Nebraska, $20-25

Touring Service map holder, 1960s
(maps not included), $40-60

Map of North Island, New Zealand, $40-50

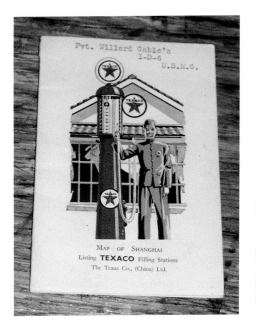

Map of Shanghai, 1936 (front cover of
map), $75-125

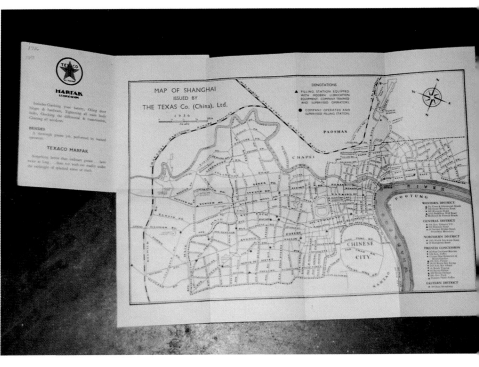

Map-Shanghai, China

MARINE

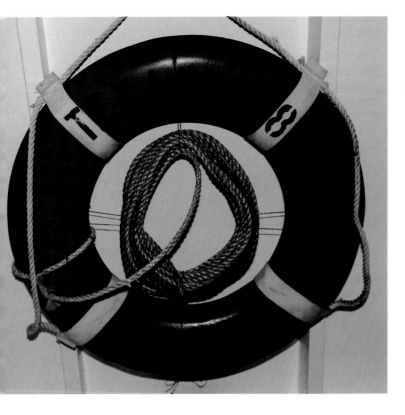

Life Preserver, $150-180

(Top sign) Red/Black, Marine Products, $550-675; (bottom sign) White, Marine Products, $550-675

Marine Lubricants (different logo), 1963, $950-1200

Marine Lubricants, 1956, $1800-2400

Marine Lubricants, 1961, $1450-1700

Small embossed pump plate, red frame, $275-350

Small embossed pump plate, gold frame, $275-350

Small pump plate, outboard blend, 18" x 12" (notice outline logo in green, very unusual), $475-600

Painted, tin Marine Lubricants, $550-700

Ink blotter 'The Fastest Boat in the World' (1933), $40-60

Display for Outboard Lubricants, $350-475(tubes and cans, $10 to $20 each)

Ink blotter 'U-10 Miss America X' (1933), $80-110

Banner 'Speed King of the World', $110-150

Display for Outboard Lubricants (larger rack), $350-475

Quart Outboard Motor Oil, $60-75

Glass, Outboard Motor Oil, $70-90

Quart Outboard Motor Oil (1940s/1950s), $175-250

Gallon Marine Motor Oil, $65-85

Quart Marine Motor Oil, $175-250
Note the difference in the boat scenes on these two cans

Gallon Marine Motor Oil (rare), $450-575

Outboard Gear Oil, $40-75

Outboard Gear Lubricant (1930s), $40-50

1957 Cruising Chart, Atlantic Coast, $55-75

(reverse side of map)

1940 Cruising Chart, Atlantic Coast, $90-110

Sky Chief Marine pump plate, 22" x 12", $175-225

Sky Chief Marine pump plate, 12" x 18", $350-425

Marine White pump plate,
8 x 12", $700-850

Mail Port, two-sided porcelain, $550-650

Marine White pump plate, 12" x 18",
curved (rare), $1400-1600

Marine White pump plate, 8" x 12",
$900-1100

Maine China Display, No Pricing
Available

Marine China, dinner plate, $110-130

Marine China, small deep dish bowl, $110-140

Marine China, salad dish, $125-145

Marine China, coffee mug, $125-140

Marine China, coffee cup, $110-130

Marine China, shaving mug (rare),
$400-600

Marine China, soup cup, $125-145

Marine China, soup bowl, $140-170

Marine China, egg cup, $275-375

Marine China, dessert bowl, $140-160

Marine China, large serving dish, $250-275

Marine China, bread plate, $90-120

Marine China, creamer, $160-190

Marine China, custard bowl, $125-150

Marine China, large platter, $225-350

Marine China, cereal bowl, $135-165

Marine China, ice cream dish, $130-150

Marine China, match holder, $275-375 (notice matchbook, $15-$20)

Marine China, small dessert bowl, $90-140

Marine China, ash tray, $200-275

Marine China, butter dish, $175-200

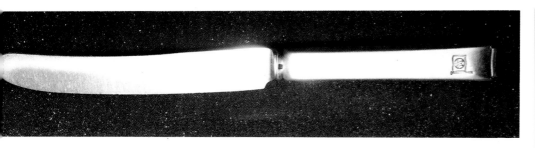

Marine China, butter knife, $60-80

Close-up of logo on knife

Porcelain dish, very early, $350-450

Marine Captain's Cap (very rare), No Pricing Available

MISCELLANEOUS PAPER PRODUCTS

Calendar, 'The Volatile Gas', 1926, $375-400

Calendar, 'lubricant for every purpose', 1923, $400-475

Car Radiator Front, 1936, waxed cardboard, $125-135

Service Station Safety Reminder, $40-60

Calendar, Safety Committees, 1928, $100-110

Salesman's Sample: Calendar and
Thermometer, 1939, $85-110

'CareLess Today...CarLess Tomorrow,
Winter Check-up Reminder, $100-125

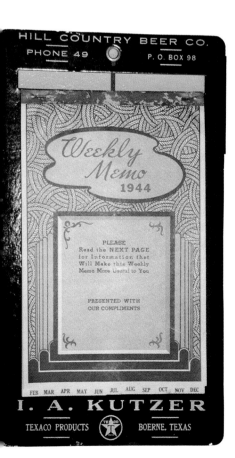

Pepsi-Cola and Texaco Display,
cardboard, $160-175

Weekly Memo Calendar, 1944, $70-80

Service Station Attendant Display, 6' cardboard, $130-145

P. T. Anti-Freeze Display, cardboard, $225-275

Santa Claus Display, 6' die-cut
cardboard, $250-300

X-Mas Window Display, cardboard,
$140-170

Credit Card Window Display, die-cut
cardboard, $60-90

'Ice-Chek' To Prevent Stalls, cardboard, $45-60

Match-book Cover Display, No Pricing Available

Match-book Cover Display, No Pricing Available

Season's Greeting from Texaco, $20-25 each

Lubrication Guides, $20-35 each

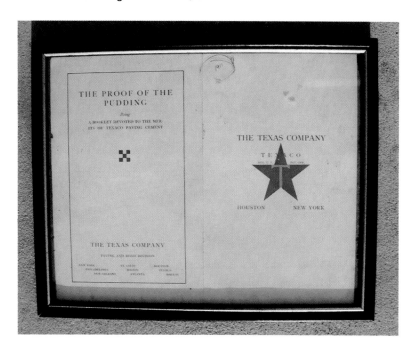

Booklet of the Merits of Texaco Paving Cement, 1911, $80-90

Gas and Oil Booklet, $60-90

Thuban
Compound
Guide, 1923,
$20-25

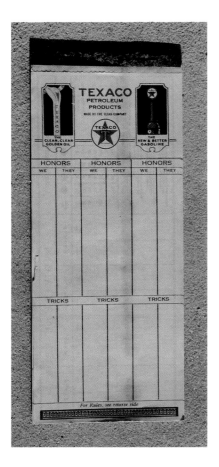

Scoring Card for Bridge Players,
$65-85

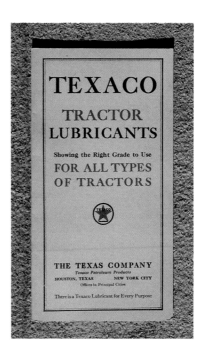

Oil Booklet for Ford Owners, $20-30

Tractor Lubricant Booklet, $20-25

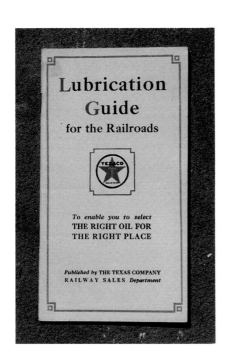

Lubricant Guide for Railroads, $20-25

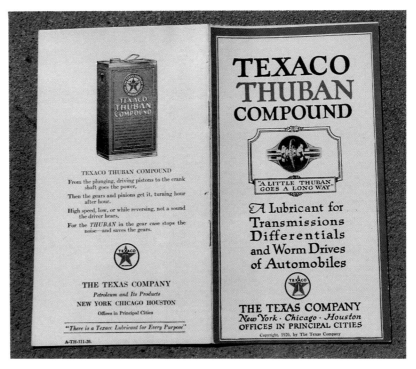

Thuban Compound Guide, 1920, $20-25

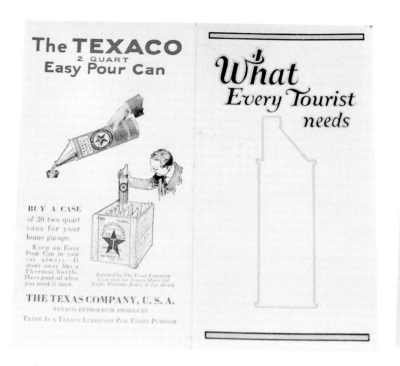

'What Every Tourist needs' brochure (outside of brochure), $65-90

Easy-Pour Can (inside of brochure)

'quick-starting, free-flowing' (outside of brochure), $75-95

For Winter Driving (inside of brochure)

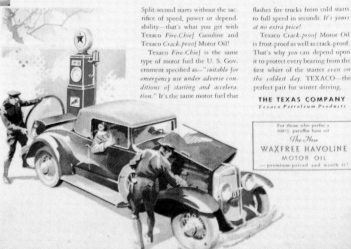

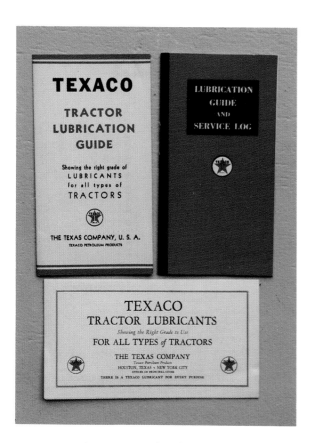

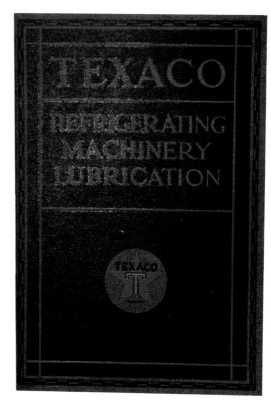

Refrigerating Machinery Lubrication Guide, $120-140

Tractor Lubrication Guides, $20-30 each

Lubrication Guide and Service Log, $30-40

Texas Star Magazine X-Mas Edition, 1915, $125-135

'At Your Service' Book of Ink Blotters (for marketing purposes),
$550-675

We Believe That We Have Rung the Bell in Advertising Value with These Blotters

In the first place they are undeniably handsome and attractive.

Secondly, they are real good blotters. They are useful. They will be kept.

Your name will appear before the eyes of a purchaser of oil and other supplies every time he uses one of them.

As before, we will furnish them free, with your name, address, and telephone number neatly printed in large type.

We ask only that you take as many as you can readily send out monthly to your prospective customers—no more, no less.

We will put them up in lots of 25, 50, 100 and more if necessary.

We know they are good advertising.

We are sure they will bring business to your place.

We are also sure that you, Mr. Dealer, will like the theme of service and economy which runs through all of them.

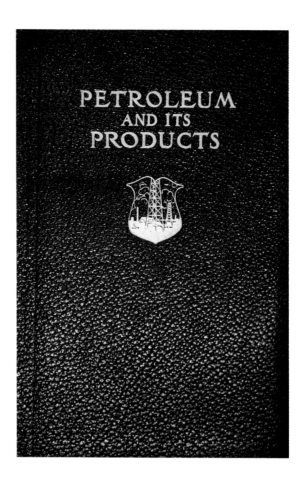

Petroleum and its Products Book, 1910, $90-110

(inside front page of book)

Book of Texaco Products, $90-120

Texaco, A Picture Story, Book, $100-150

Can and Packaging Plant—Port Arthur, Texas

Can Processing

Program from First Annual Stamp Exhibition, $25-30

Modern Packaging Pamphlet, 1935,
$150-175

'Signed, Sealed, Delivered', page from
book

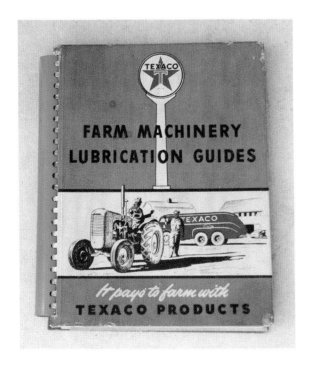

Farm Machinery Lubrication Guides,
$80-140

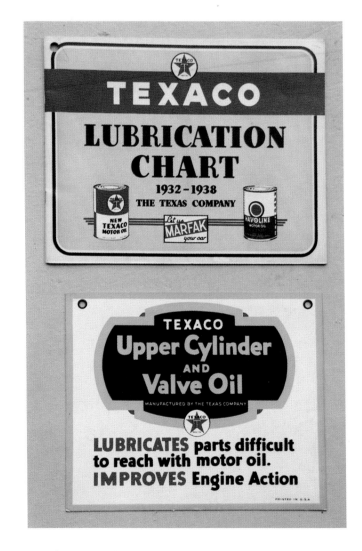

Lubrication Chart, 1932-38, $30-40;
Upper Cylinder and Valve Oil, $50-60

Painted Bulletin Designs, for Texaco
Dealers, 1938, $75-95

(page from book)

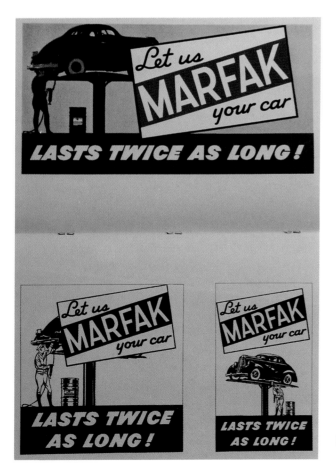

Texaco Dealer Magazine, 1947, $50-75

(page from book)

Texaco Helps (booklet for Texaco Dealers), $225-250

Signs That Show the Way to Profits
(page from booklet)

Grades of Gasoline (page from booklet)

Lubrication Cabinet (page from booklet)

Dealer Marketing Tools, 1955, $100-125

(reverse side)

Texaco Dealer Magazine, 1953, $50-75

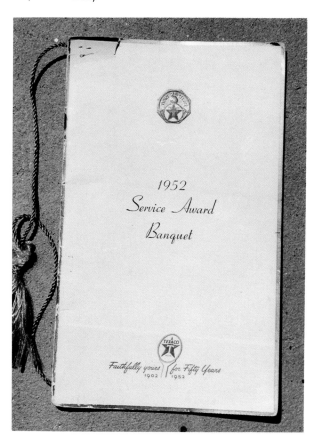

Service Award Banquet, 1952 (50-year
Anniversary), $120-135

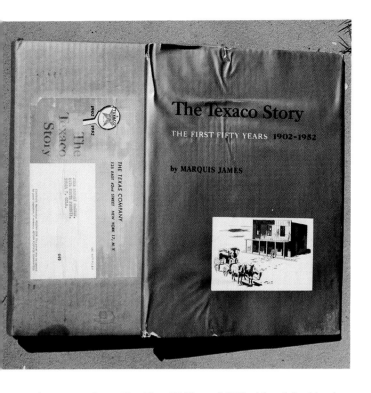

The Texaco Story, The First 50 Years (NOS with original box),
$100-125 (NOS only)

Texaco Annual Report, 1952, $30-40

Texaco Star Employee Magazine, 1977, 75th Anniversary
Edition, $100-125

Texaco Marketer Magazine, 75th
Anniversary, $100-125

Paper Kite, $10-20

Dealer Order Form, No Pricing Available

Bear Decals, $25-40 each

Post Card, $40-50

Post Card, $40-50

ROOFING PRODUCTS

Coatings and Cements, one-sided, painted metal (1920-30s),
$1500-1700

Ink Blotter, $100-150

Advertising Mailer, $15-20

Roofing Cement and Asphalt Roof
Coating Cans, $100-175 each

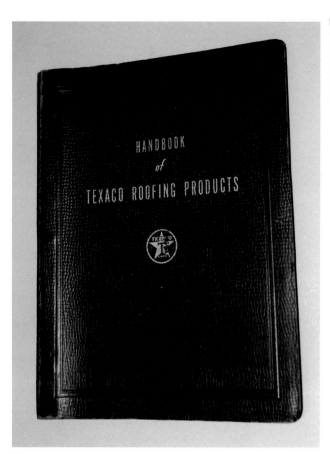

Roofing Products Handbook, $100-140

Literature inside of Handbook

Asphalt Shingles Display Board, one-sided porcelain, $650-800

Wooden section of Packing Crate for Hexagon Strip Shingles, $75-100

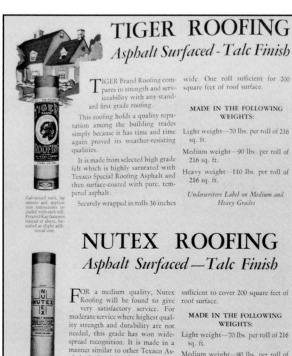

TIGER ROOFING
Asphalt Surfaced - Talc Finish

TIGER Brand Roofing compares in strength and serviceability with any standard first grade roofing.

This roofing holds a quality reputation among the building trades simply because it has time and time again proved its weather-resisting qualities.

It is made from selected high grade felt which is highly saturated with Texaco Special Roofing Asphalt and then surface-coated with pure, tempered asphalt.

Securely wrapped in rolls 36 inches

wide. One roll sufficient for 200 square feet of roof surface.

MADE IN THE FOLLOWING WEIGHTS:

Light weight—70 lbs. per roll of 216 sq. ft.

Medium weight—90 lbs. per roll of 216 sq. ft.

Heavy weight—110 lbs. per roll of 216 sq. ft.

Underwriters Label on Medium and Heavy Grades

Galvanized nails, lap cement and application instructions included with each roll. Pyramid Kap fasteners instead of above, furnished at slight additional cost.

NUTEX ROOFING
Asphalt Surfaced — Talc Finish

FOR a medium quality, Nutex Roofing will be found to give very satisfactory service. For moderate service where highest quality strength and durability are not needed, this grade has won widespread recognition. It is made in a manner similar to other Texaco Asphalt Surfaced Roofings, with felt base saturated with Texaco Special Roofing Asphalt, and finished with an asphalt surface coating and talc. Nutex Roofing is securely wrapped in rolls 36 inches wide, each roll

sufficient to cover 200 square feet of roof surface.

MADE IN THE FOLLOWING WEIGHTS:

Light weight—70 lbs. per roll of 216 sq. ft.

Medium weight—90 lbs. per roll of 216 sq. ft.

Heavy weight—110 lbs. per roll of 216 sq. ft.

Underwriters Label on Medium and Heavy Grades

Ungalvanized nails, lap cement and application instructions included with each roll.

Advertising Page from Handbook

Asphalt Shingles and Roofing sign (24 x 54), one-sided porcelain (1936), $550-625

Asphalt Shingles and Roofing sign (16 x 36), one-sided painted metal (1936), $475-550

Slate Surfaced Shingles Pamphlet, $40-50

Wooden section of Packing Crate, for Strip Shingles, $75-100

Roofing Material, salesman's sample,
$250-300

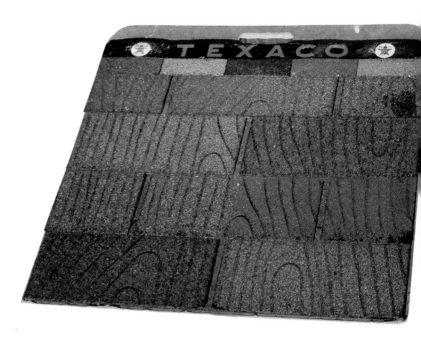

Roofing Material, salesman's sample,
$250-300

Liquid Roofing Cement, one gallon,
$275-350

Roofing Nail Apron, $75-110

TOYS

Toy Tanker with Stand, NOS in box, "Have Fun" booklet included, $300-375

Toy Tanker advertising piece, $75-100

Fire Chief Speaker Hat advertising piece, $75-100

Kid's Fire Chief Hat, $40-60

Kid's Fire Chief Hat, $40-60

Danny O'Day Doll, $325-475

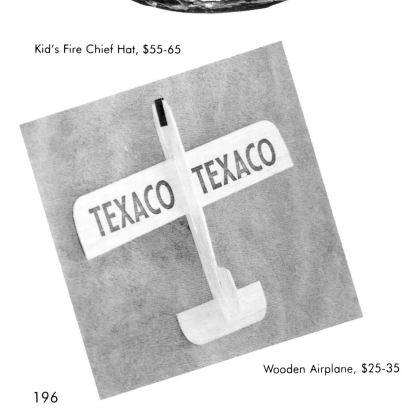

Kid's Fire Chief Hat, $55-65

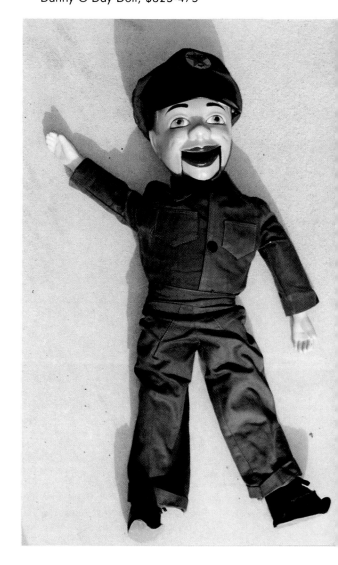

Wooden Airplane, $25-35

Tanker Truck, pressed tin, $90-120

Toy Race Car, $60-75

Filling Station Toy, pressed tin, $575-625

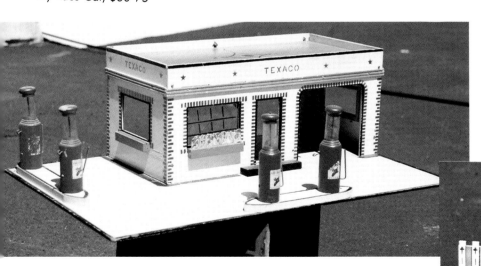

One-bay Station (Rich toy), $600-675

Small Gas Station (Rich toy), $475-550

Tanker Truck, cast, $60-80

Silver Tanker Truck, cast, $70-90

Tanker Truck, cast, $70-90

Tanker Truck, cast, $60-90

Tanker Truck, cast, $80-90

Tanker Truck, cast, $175-200

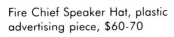

Northrop Gamma Plane and Box
(plastic kit), $125-145

Fire Chief Speaker Hat, plastic
advertising piece, $60-70

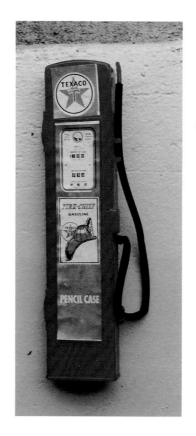

Gas Pump Pencil Case, $90-100

Gas Pump Bank, plastic, $175-200

#2 Bank, cast-iron (NOS), No Pricing
Available

#1 Bank, cast-iron (NOS), No Pricing Available

#3 Bank, cast-iron (NOS), No Pricing
Available

Buddy L Highway Set (NOS), $125-140

Fire Chief Speaker Hat advertising piece, with hat and box (NOS), $240-260

Roadway Sign, Salesman's Sample, $275-350

Tanker Truck, cast-iron, $175-200

Mac Tanker Truck, plastic, $250-280

Texaco Star Race Car, plastic (1960s),
$70-85

Texaco Star Race Car, plastic (1980s), $70-85

Havoline Car driven by Davey Allison,
No Pricing Available

Tanker Truck (NOS) in box (1950s),
$275-300

Emergency Truck, rare (1950s), No
Pricing Available

Truck, $55-60

Fire Truck (late 1950s), $220-250

Fire Truck, (NOS) in box (1960s), $175-250

Tanker Truck, (NOS) in box (1970s),
$125-150

Texaco Station (1960s), $175-250

Gasoline Station, pressed tin (former
USSR), No Pricing Available

Pump Display (front, Jack Benny), $45-55

(reverse 'Fill It Up, Jack')

Texaco Star Theater starring Milton
Berle, $100-125

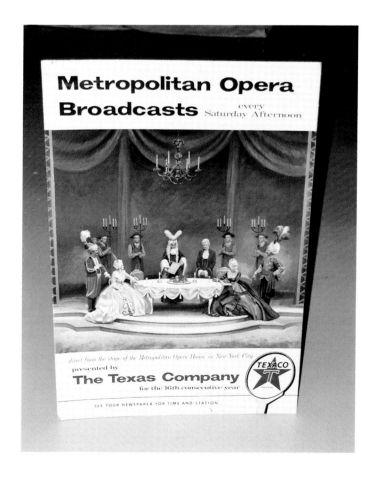

Metropolitan Opera Broadcasts presented by Texaco,
$100-150

Ed Wynn Mask, signed, $300-375

Ed Wynn Bust (may be one-of-a-kind),
$1000-1200

Ed Wynn Puzzle, signed, $250-300

Ed Wynn Fire Chief Puzzle, signed, $90-120

Ed Wynn Poster, $40-60

'Swing Into Spring' by Benny Goodman, 45 rpm record, $145-200

Danny O'Day Hand Puppet, $75-100

Danny O'Day Puppet, Record and Instructions (NOS), $850-1000 (NOS only)

QUICK REFERENCE SERVICE GUIDE

Sales and Service:

Rick Pease
3705 Pecan Park Drive
Weatherford, Texas 76087
(817) 596-9328
Globes, Oil Cans, and Signs
Buys and Sells

Kim and Mary Kokles
P.O. Box 475092
Garland, Texas 75047
(972)240-1987
Buys and Sells
Collects all Types of Antique Advertising

Erol Tuzcu
3400 West 45th Street
West Palm Beach, Florida 33407
(800) 273-6181
Collector

Oil Company Collectibles
Scott Benjamin, owner
411 Forest Street
LaGrange, Ohio 44050
(216) 355-6608
Original Globes and Signs
Buys and Sells

Howard Clayburn
8903 Alcott
Houston, Texas 77080
(713)461-4296
Buys and Sells
Signs, Cans, Globes

Gasoline Pump Parts
Bob Bardwell, owner
P. O. Box 771
Burton, Texas 77835
(409) 289-5501
Pump Restoration
Gas Pump Parts
Decals
Buys and Sells

Vick's Place
Vick and Sara Raupe, owners
124 No. 2nd
Guthrie, Oklahoma 73044
(405) 282-5586
Pump Restoration
Gas Pump Parts
Globes, Signs, Decals

Ron Scobie
7676 120th Street No.
Hugo, Minnesota 55038
(612) 426-1023
New Dial Faces
Air Meter Parts
Gas Pump Parts

Michael Slama
122 NW 10th Avenue
Portland, Oregon 97209
(503) 228-8347
Gas Pump Parts
Decals
Pump Restoration

Shaver's Restoration Shop
Charles Shaver, owner
Rt. 1
Liberal, Missouri 64762
(417) 394-2788
Pump Restoration
Gas Pump Parts

Bob Hull
31680 Mills Road
Avon, Ohio 44011
(216) 327-6097
Pump Restoration
Gas Pump Parts

Park Drive Garage
Andy Anderson, owner
5734 So. 86th Circle
Omaha, Nebraska 68127
(402) 592-1710
Gas Pump Parts
Decals

New Globes, Signs, Decals, Nostalgia Items:

Lee Pergal
10985 Woodstock Road
Roswell, Georgia 30075
(770) 587-1822

Time Passages
Scott and Debbie Anderson
P. O. Box 65596
West DesMoines, Iowa 50265
(800) 383-8888

Webers Nostalgia Supermarket
6611 Anglin Drive
Fort Worth, Texas 76119
(817) 534-6611

Magazine Publications for Collectors:

Check The Oil
P. O. Box 937
Powell, Ohio 43065-0937
(800) 228-6624 or (614) 848-5038
(614) 436-4760 fax

Petroleum Collectibles Monthly
411 Forest Street
LaGrange, Ohio 44050
(216) 355-6608
(216) 355-4955 fax

Mobilia
P. O. Box 575
Middlebury, Vermont 05753
(802) 388-3071 ext. 21
(802) 388-2215 fax

Auction Services:

Autopia
Win Maynard
15209 NE 90th Street
Redmond, Washington 98052
(206) 883-7653
(206) 867-5568 fax

Collectors Auction Services
Mark Anderton
Rt. 2 Box 431 Oakwood Road
Oil City, Pennsylvania 16301
(814) 677-6070
(814) 677-6166 fax

Wm Moreford
RD #2
Cazenovia, New York 13035
(315) 662-7625